TOUCHPOINTS FOR LEADERS

Other TouchPoints Products:

TouchPoint Bible
TouchPoints
TouchPoints for Women
TouchPoints for Men
TouchPoints for Students
TouchPoints for Couples
TouchPoints for Hurting People
TouchPoint Bible Promises
TouchPoints of Hope
TouchPoints for Troubled Times

TouchPoints
FOR LEADERS

GOD'S WISDOM FOR
LEADING IN LIFE, FAMILY,
WORK, AND MINISTRY

Tyndale House Publishers, Inc.
Wheaton, Illinois

Visit Tyndale's exciting Web site at www.tyndale.com

General editors: Ronald A. Beers and V. Gilbert Beers

Written and compiled by Douglas J. Rumford

Contributing writers: V. Gilbert Beers, Ronald A. Beers, Brian R. Coffey, Jonathan D. Gray, Shawn A. Harrison, Sanford D. Hull, Rhonda K. O'Brien.

Designed by Timothy R. Botts

Edited by Linda K. Taylor

ISBN 0-8423-5130-2

Printed in the United States of America

09 08 07 06 05
8 7 6 5

PREFACE

A LEADER'S LIFE is complex—involving head and heart, skills and competencies, character and spiritual values. Effective leadership is driven by inner motivation, not outward incentives. Yes, there are desires for success, for impact, and for recognition. But countless leaders testify that the intangible satisfactions matter more to them than the things they can measure on a spreadsheet.

TouchPoints for Leaders has been compiled with this perspective on leaders and leadership. We have all sorts of leadership situations in view. Leaders are, most simply, *people with influence*. This influence can be formal (as in a work situation between an employer and employee) or more informal (as in the influences we have on friends, family, and in our various social relationships). Leaders can be the teachers up front in the classroom, or the students to whom other students look. They can be the foremen at the manufacturing plant or the worker who brings spark and energy to the workplace. Leaders are parents in the home, neighbors in the community, members of a church, and employers and employees in the world of work.

These verses and comments, which are arranged alphabetically by topic, are not simply about a leader's activities, but more about a leader's inner life. We explore the dynamics and challenges that leaders face within themselves, in interpersonal relationships, in their leadership settings, and in light of the culture around them. We see how our spiritual walk with God is at the heart of everything, including what many would call the "secular" aspects of their work. While many of the Scriptures apply more directly to spiritual leadership, it is a fairly easy transition to apply them to leadership in other areas.

Now as always, God is looking for leaders who will be people "after his own heart" (1 Samuel 13:14). May *TouchPoints for Leaders* be a tool in God's hand to shape us as leaders in homes, congregations, communities, and the world.

—DOUGLAS J. RUMFORD

2 Timothy 3:16-17 *All Scripture is inspired by God and is useful to teach us what is true and to make us realize what is wrong in our lives. It straightens us out and teaches us to do what is right. It is God's way of preparing us in every way, fully equipped for every good thing God wants us to do.*

ABILITIES

See also **STEWARDSHIP**

Where do my abilities come from?

Deuteronomy 8:18 *Always remember that it is the Lord your God who gives you power to become rich, and he does it to fulfill the covenant he made with your ancestors.*

Exodus 31:1-3 *The Lord also said to Moses, "Look, I have chosen Bezalel son of Uri, grandson of Hur, of the tribe of Judah. I have filled him with the Spirit of God, giving him great wisdom, intelligence, and skill in all kinds of crafts."*

John 15:5 *For apart from me you can do nothing.*

1 Corinthians 4:7 *What makes you better than anyone else? What do you have that God hasn't given you? And if all you have is from God, why boast as though you have accomplished something on your own?*

Leaders must remember that there are no self-made people. God gives you the abilities to accomplish your responsibilities and to provide for your needs. You are a steward of your talents and will answer to the Lord for what you have done with them.

What does God expect me to do with my abilities?

Matthew 25:29 *To those who use well what they are given, even more will be given, and they will have an abundance. But from those who are unfaithful, even what little they have will be taken away.*
God has entrusted resources to you according to your ability. He expects you to maximize the effectiveness of those abilities in proportion to his gifting. While the most talented leaders may seem the most blessed, they must also be the most responsible.

John 17:4 *I brought glory to you here on earth by doing everything you told me to do.*
Jesus' mission in life was pleasing the Father. This is the ultimate purpose of every leader. Like Jesus, you are called to bring glory to God through all you say and do—in all times, places, and circumstances.

How can my abilities and even my successes be a danger?

Deuteronomy 8:11-14 *Beware that in your plenty you do not forget the Lord your God and disobey his commands, regulations, and laws. For when you have become full and prosperous and have built fine homes to live in, and when your flocks and herds have become very large and your silver and gold have multiplied along with everything else, that is the time to be careful. Do not become proud at that time and forget the Lord your God.*
When your ability brings you good success and blessing, you are in danger of falling into complacency and forgetting that God gave you your abilities and that you are to consistently use them to serve him and others. Another danger of having great ability is to think you no longer need help or advice from others.

1 Corinthians 1:26-29 *Remember, dear brothers and sisters, that few of you were wise in the world's eyes, or powerful, or wealthy when God called you. Instead, God deliberately chose things the world considers foolish in order to shame those who think they are wise. And he chose those who are powerless to shame those who are powerful. God chose things despised by the world, things counted as nothing at all, and used them to bring to nothing what the world considers important, so that no one can ever boast in the presence of God.*
Your abilities can be liabilities. Within each ability lie the seeds of problems that will sprout if you neglect that ability, use it for your own selfish designs, or presume to rely on it apart from the Lord.

Do my limited abilities limit my ability to serve God?
2 Chronicles 20:12 *O our God, won't you stop them? We are powerless against this mighty army that is about to attack us. We do not know what to do, but we are looking to you for help.*
Jehoshaphat, king of Judah, was overwhelmed by the attack coming against the nation because he knew his abilities and resources were no match against the enemies. But God opened the way to success. Leaders understand that availability and dependence on the Lord are as important as ability.

Psalm 147:10-11 *The strength of a horse does not impress him; how puny in his sight is the strength of a man. Rather, the Lord's delight is in those who honor him, those who put their hope in his unfailing love.*
God is not impressed by your abilities or your resources, but by your faith in him.

Zechariah 4:6 *It is not by force nor by strength, but by my Spirit, says the Lord Almighty.*
When facing the most threatening obstacles, the Lord

assures you that his ability, not your own, is the ultimate assurance of success.

PROMISE FROM GOD Luke 12:48 *Much is required from those to whom much is given, and much more is required from those to whom much more is given.*

ACCEPT/ACCEPTANCE

See also **APPROVAL**

What is the basis for my acceptance as a leader?

Matthew 3:16-17 *After his baptism, as Jesus came up out of the water, the heavens were opened and he saw the Spirit of God descending like a dove and settling on him. And a voice from heaven said, "This is my beloved Son, and I am fully pleased with him."*

Romans 5:1-2 *Therefore, since we have been made right in God's sight by faith, we have peace with God because of what Jesus Christ our Lord has done for us. Because of our faith, Christ has brought us into this place of highest privilege where we now stand, and we confidently and joyfully look forward to sharing God's glory.*

Jesus was blessed and accepted by God because of who he was, not because of what he did. Many leaders assume that performance is the means to acceptance. They are driven to earn respect from others, to impress others, to gain the applause and approval of others. This can easily transfer over to their relationship with God—thinking they have to earn his love and acceptance, too. But you are accepted by grace, not because of performance. God accepts you from the start, before you have accomplished great things.

What is the basis for me to accept others?

Romans 15:7 *So accept each other just as Christ has accepted you; then God will be glorified.*

1 Samuel 22:2 *Then others began coming—men who were in trouble or in debt or who were just discontented—until David was the leader of about four hundred men.*

Leaders have a great deal of influence on how others are treated. Leaders should use that influence positively to accept others for who they are as people. Welcome others in the Spirit of Christ, not because of position, prestige, power, or personal gain that may come your way. David modeled this acceptance of others as he was fleeing from Saul. As a developing leader, David learned that it wasn't simply a matter of getting the best people, but of bringing out the best in the people God brought to him.

PROMISE FROM GOD Romans 8:39 *Nothing . . . will ever be able to separate us from the love of God that is revealed in Christ Jesus our Lord.*

ACCOUNTABILITY

See also **PARTNERSHIP**

How are we all held accountable?

Romans 14:7-8, 12 *For we are not our own masters when we live or when we die. While we live, we live to please the Lord. And when we die, we go to be with the Lord. So in life and in death, we belong to the Lord. . . . Yes, each of us will have to give a personal account to God.*

2 Corinthians 5:9-10 *So our aim is to please him always, whether we are here in this body or away from*

this body. For we must all stand before Christ to be judged. We will each receive whatever we deserve for the good or evil we have done in our bodies.

We must all live today as though we will be in eternity tomorrow. Because you are saved by Christ through faith, you are to lead a life of gratitude that you have been given eternal life, and of obedience to the standards by which Christ lived. You will one day have to give an account for what you did with all God gave you.

Are leaders held to a different standard of accountability?

Jeremiah 23:1-2 *"I will send disaster upon the leaders of my people—the shepherds of my sheep—for they have destroyed and scattered the very ones they were expected to care for," says the Lord. This is what the Lord, the God of Israel, says to these shepherds: "Instead of leading my flock to safety, you have deserted them and driven them to destruction. Now I will pour out judgment on you for the evil you have done to them."*

Hebrews 13:17 *Obey your spiritual leaders and do what they say. Their work is to watch over your souls, and they know they are accountable to God. Give them reason to do this joyfully and not with sorrow.*

James 3:1 *Dear brothers and sisters, not many of you should become teachers in the church, for we who teach will be judged by God with greater strictness.*

One of the mistakes leaders make is thinking they are somehow exceptions to the rule, exempted from the standards that apply to everyone else. However, quite the opposite is true. In fact, leaders are held to even higher standards, especially when others are depending on them for direction and support. You need to be aware that with your great influence comes great responsibility.

What can I do to reinforce obedience and keep myself from disobedience?

Mark 6:7 *And he called his twelve disciples together and sent them out two by two.*

Galatians 6:1-2 *Dear brothers and sisters, if another Christian is overcome by some sin, you who are godly should gently and humbly help that person back onto the right path. And be careful not to fall into the same temptation yourself. Share each other's troubles and problems, and in this way obey the law of Christ*

Jesus created accountability by sending his disciples out in pairs. Leaders should model this practice in their own lives as well in their organizing of others. You should encourage and establish relationships with others who will call you to maintain your standards and agree to keep a check on your conduct.

PROMISE FROM GOD 1 John 2:3 *How can we be sure that we belong to him? By obeying his commandments.*

ACCUSATIONS

See also **CRITICISM**

Why are accusations made against me and my leadership?

Psalm 7:1-2 *I come to you for protection, O Lord my God. Save me from my persecutors—rescue me! If you don't, they will maul me like a lion, tearing me to pieces with no one to rescue me.*

Psalm 35:11 *Malicious witnesses testify against me. They accuse me of things I don't even know about.*

John 15:18-19 *When the world hates you, remember it hated me before it hated you. The world would love you if you belonged to it, but you don't. I chose you to come out of the world, and so it hates you.*

As a leader, you are in the public view and are likely to be accused unjustly and blamed for circumstances and events over which you have no control. Don't be surprised when this happens. Since Jesus himself was falsely accused, his followers can expect similar treatment.

Where do accusations come from?

Ephesians 6:12 *For we are not fighting against people made of flesh and blood, but against the evil rulers and authorities of the unseen world, against those mighty powers of darkness who rule this world, and against wicked spirits in the heavenly realms.*

Revelation 12:10 *Then I heard a loud voice shouting across the heavens, "It has happened at last—the salvation and power and kingdom of our God, and the authority of his Christ! For the Accuser has been thrown down to earth—the one who accused our brothers and sisters before our God day and night."*

Spiritual forces of darkness are often working through and behind much of the criticism and antagonism you face.

How should I respond to accusations?

Psalm 27:1-3 *The Lord is my light and my salvation—so why should I be afraid? The Lord protects me from danger—so why should I tremble? When evil people come to destroy me, when my enemies and foes attack me, they will stumble and fall. Though a mighty army surrounds me, my heart will know no fear. Even if they attack me, I remain confident.*

Romans 8:31 *If God is for us, who can ever be against us?*

Your first line of defense is to draw strength from the assurance that God is for you, not against you. Human accusation, criticism, and opposition cannot quench the fortifying power of God's love and affirmation.

Psalm 119:78 *Bring disgrace upon the arrogant people who lied about me; meanwhile, I will concentrate on your commandments.*

Proverbs 26:2 *Like a fluttering sparrow or a darting swallow, an unfair curse will not land on its intended victim.*

1 Peter 2:15 *It is God's will that your good lives should silence those who make foolish accusations against you.*

Undeserved and false accusations will eventually be exposed for what they really are. As a leader, do not waste time planning how to even the score with those who accuse you. Focus instead on the instructions and promises of God's Word. Seek to live a godly lifestyle that will silence foolish accusations.

Romans 12:14-21 *If people persecute you because you are a Christian, don't curse them; pray that God will bless them. . . . Never pay back evil for evil to anyone. . . . Never avenge yourselves. Leave that to God. . . . Instead, do what the Scriptures say: "If your enemies are hungry, feed them. If they are thirsty, give them something to drink, and they will be ashamed of what they have done to you." Don't let evil get the best of you, but conquer evil by doing good.*

Jude 9 *But even Michael, one of the mightiest of the angels, did not dare accuse Satan of blasphemy, but simply said, "The Lord rebuke you."*
While you may be tempted to exercise your power and influence to justify yourself and vindicate your reputation, remember that the best course of action is trusting the Lord to make things right.

PROMISE FROM GOD Romans 8:33-34 *Who dares accuse us whom God has chosen for his own? Will God? No! He is the one who has given us right standing with himself. Who then will condemn us? Will Christ Jesus? No, for he is the one who died for us and was raised to life for us and is sitting at the place of highest honor next to God, pleading for us.*

ACHIEVEMENTS

See also **SUCCESS**

What does God expect me to achieve through my leadership role?

John 14:12-14 *The truth is, anyone who believes in me will do the same works I have done, and even greater works, because I am going to be with the Father. You can ask for anything in my name, and I will do it, because the work of the Son brings glory to the Father. Yes, ask anything in my name, and I will do it!*

John 15:16 *You didn't choose me. I chose you. I appointed you to go and produce fruit that will last, so that the Father will give you whatever you ask for, using my name.*

Ephesians 2:10 *For we are God's masterpiece. He has created us anew in Christ Jesus, so that we can do the*

good things he planned for us long ago.
A leader has been created, called, and equipped to serve God in significant ways. Your achievements, however, are always to be understood as the fruit of God's grace in you, not the result of your own efforts. Your greatest accomplishment is allowing God to carry out his plans through you.

What are the dangers of achievements?

Genesis 11:2-4 *As the people migrated eastward, they found a plain in the land of Babylonia and settled there. They began to talk about construction projects. "Come," they said, "let's make great piles of burnt brick and collect natural asphalt to use as mortar. Let's build a great city with a tower that reaches to the skies—a monument to our greatness!"*
Leaders are committed to significant achievements. The construction of the Tower of Babel, however, warns about pursuing such achievements solely for personal advancement. Achievements are meant to glorify God, not to be the means for achieving your own fame.

2 Chronicles 26:14-16 *Uzziah provided the entire army with shields, spears, helmets, coats of mail, bows, and sling stones. . . . His fame spread far and wide, for the Lord helped him wonderfully until he became very powerful. But when he had become powerful, he also became proud, which led to his downfall.*
Uzziah's success led to presumption and sin. The very achievements that God allows and enables can stir the pride that might draw you away from God and seduce you into disobedience.

Amos 6:4-7 *How terrible it will be for you who sprawl on ivory beds surrounded with luxury, eating the meat of tender lambs and choice calves. You sing idle songs to the sound of the harp, and you fancy yourselves to be great musicians, as King David was. You drink wine by the bowlful, and you perfume yourselves with exotic fragrances, caring nothing at all that your nation is going to ruin. Therefore, you will be the first to be led away as captives. Suddenly, all your revelry will end.*

Your achievements cannot protect you from the consequences of selfish indulgence and injustice. As a leader, you dare not allow success to insulate you from the welfare of the people God has called you to lead.

How am I to view my achievements?

James 1:9-11 *Christians who are poor should be glad, for God has honored them. And those who are rich should be glad, for God has humbled them. They will fade away like a flower in the field. The hot sun rises and dries up the grass; the flower withers, and its beauty fades away. So also, wealthy people will fade away with all of their achievements.*

There can be joy in poverty or in wealth. Most of your accomplishments don't last and will soon be forgotten. That's why God's love is not based on your achievements, but on his own choice to love you and cherish you. Accomplishments that last are those that are done with an eternal perspective in mind.

PROMISE FROM GOD Psalm 60:12 *With God's help we will do mighty things.*

ADMINISTRATION

See **ORGANIZATION**

ADVICE/ADVISERS

See also **COUNSEL/COUNSELORS/DECISIONS**

Why is it important for me to get good advice?

Proverbs 12:15 *Fools think they need no advice, but the wise listen to others.*

Proverbs 13:14 *The advice of the wise is like a life-giving fountain; those who accept it avoid the snares of death.*

Proverbs 15:22 *Plans go wrong for lack of advice; many counselors bring success.*

Proverbs 19:20 *Get all the advice and instruction you can, and be wise the rest of your life.*

Leaders need good advisers who bring expertise, perspective, and experience to the challenges and problems they face. No one is wise enough or perceptive enough to grasp the full meaning and possibilities of a situation. The right counsel can make the difference between success and failure, prosperity and poverty, victory and defeat.

How can good advice benefit everyone?

Exodus 18:14-19 *When Moses' father-in-law saw all that Moses was doing for the people, he said, "Why are you trying to do all this alone? The people have been standing here all day to get your help. . . . This is not good!" his father-in-law exclaimed. "You're going to wear yourself out—and the people, too. This job is too heavy a burden for you to handle all by yourself. Now let me give you a word of advice, and may God be with you."*

The best advice can help everybody involved in a situation. Jethro's advice benefited Moses and the entire nation. Moses was able to live with a more manageable load of responsibility, others were trained to participate in leadership, and the people were served in a more timely and equitable manner.

What happens if I ignore good advice?

1 Kings 12:8 *But Rehoboam rejected the advice of the elders and instead asked the opinion of the young men who had grown up with him and who were now his advisers.*
Leaders must evaluate all advice in light of its faithfulness to biblical principles and its impact on God's people. Rehoboam desired to assert his power instead of showing appropriate authority in a compassionate manner. His rejection of the advice of wise men led to civil war, splitting Israel from that time forward.

PROMISE FROM GOD Psalm 32:8 *I will guide you along the best pathway for your life. I will advise you and watch over you.*

AMBITION

See also **PRIDE**

Is ambition ever appropriate?

Romans 15:20 *My ambition has always been to preach the Good News where the name of Christ has never been heard, rather than where a church has already been started by someone else.*
Paul demonstrated a "holy ambition" to do great things for God. Unholy ambition attempts only to advance one's own reputation and cause. Holy ambition, however, means to offer oneself to be used by God to advance *his* reputation and *his* cause. A holy

ambition is a large vision rooted in the will and service of God—a cause so large only God can pull it off.

1 Thessalonians 4:11-12 *This should be your ambition: to live a quiet life, minding your own business and working with your hands, just as we commanded you before. As a result, people who are not Christians will respect the way you live, and you will not need to depend on others to meet your financial needs.*
A fundamental ambition in life is to provide for yourself so that you will be respected by others and not be a burden to them.

What are some of the dangers of ambition?
Galatians 5:19-20 *When you follow the desires of your sinful nature, your lives will produce these evil results: . . . selfish ambition.*

James 3:16 *For wherever there is jealousy and selfish ambition, there you will find disorder and every kind of evil.*
Ambition arises from your sinful nature and can fuel not only your sinful behavior but also conflict with others. Ambition cuts you off from the Holy Spirit, putting your agenda and self-gratification ahead of God's will for you.

Mark 8:34-37 *Then he called his disciples and the crowds to come over and listen. "If any of you wants to be my follower," he told them, "you must put aside your selfish ambition, shoulder your cross, and follow me. If you try to keep your life for yourself, you will lose it. But if you give up your life for my sake and for the sake of the Good News, you will find true life. And how do you benefit if you gain the whole world but lose your own soul in the process? Is anything worth more than your soul?"*
There is a difference between being a part of God's great work and wanting personal greatness through

God's work. It's the difference between serving God and desiring God to serve you. Ambition can fool you into striving to gain the whole world at the cost of your spiritual welfare.

How can I guard against ambition?

Philippians 2:3 *Don't be selfish; don't live to make a good impression on others. Be humble, thinking of others as better than yourself.*
Your priorities change when you think of others instead of worrying about how others think of you. Rather than trying to impress others that you are better than you are, your call is to impress others with their worth and value in Christ.

Philippians 3:8, 13-14 *Yes, everything else is worthless when compared with the priceless gain of knowing Christ Jesus my Lord. . . . I am focusing all my energies on this one thing: Forgetting the past and looking forward to what lies ahead, I strain to reach the end of the race and receive the prize for which God, through Christ Jesus, is calling us up to heaven.*
Ambition fades as the true perception of reality dawns. In reality, your earthly achievements cannot compare with knowing Jesus Christ. In fact, they can get in the way, distracting you from depending fully on God. At the end of your life, only what's done for him will matter.

PROMISE FROM GOD Psalm 37:4 *Take delight in the Lord, and he will give you your heart's desires.*

ANGER

See also **CONFLICT**

How does anger impact my effectiveness as a leader?

Numbers 20:10-12 *"Listen, you rebels!" [Moses] shouted. "Must we bring you water from this rock?" Then Moses raised his hand and struck the rock twice with the staff, and water gushed out. . . . But the Lord said to Moses and Aaron, "Because you did not trust me enough to demonstrate my holiness to the people of Israel, you will not lead them into the land I am giving them!"*

Proverbs 14:29 *Those who control their anger have great understanding; those with a hasty temper will make mistakes.*

A leader's patience is often tried to the limits. The persistent complaints and blame of the people drove Moses to anger. Even when God gave the assurance of providing water, Moses could not restrain his anger and deliberately disobeyed God. Moses' anger cost him the fulfillment of his mission to enter the Promised Land. Failure to restrain your anger may mean failure to realize your God-given dreams.

Matthew 5:21-22 *You have heard that the law of Moses says, "Do not murder. If you commit murder, you are subject to judgment." But I say, if you are angry with someone, you are subject to judgment!*

Anger harms others and yourself more than you realize. Anger brings judgment against you because it is an attack on people created in God's image. A leader's primary call is to value people, not curse them.

Is anger ever appropriate?

John 2:15-16 *[Jesus] drove out the sheep and oxen, scattered the money changers' coins . . . , and . . . told them, "Get these things out of here. Don't turn my Father's house into a marketplace!"*

Mark 3:5 *He looked around at them angrily, because he was deeply disturbed by their hard hearts.*
Jesus' righteous anger arose from his devotion to God and compassion for others. Unrighteous anger is rooted in pride and self-interest.

How should I deal with my own anger in relationships?

Ephesians 4:26-27 *And "don't sin by letting anger gain control over you." Don't let the sun go down while you are still angry, for anger gives a mighty foothold to the Devil.*
Learning to bring your emotions under the Holy Spirit's control is part of the process of spiritual maturity. Anger can either be an emotional response that can be managed for productive results or a volatile reaction that hurts and destroys. When you feel anger rising, you can train yourself to examine your heart: Who is really offended in this situation? Is this about God's honor or my pride? When you fail (which may be often), you should confess, forgive, and seek reconciliation. Allowing anger to linger leaves the door open to many sins.

Proverbs 25:23 *As surely as a wind from the north brings rain, so a gossiping tongue causes anger!*
Leaders must guard their speech, especially their comments about others. Criticism or casual remarks are often retold, sparking hurt and anger in their wake. Wise leaders share only those comments they won't mind having quoted to any and all.

What are the benefits of restraining my anger?
Proverbs 15:1 *A gentle answer turns away wrath, but harsh words stir up anger.*

Proverbs 19:11 *People with good sense restrain their anger; they earn esteem by overlooking wrongs.*

Proverbs 29:11 *A fool gives full vent to anger, but a wise person quietly holds it back.*
Rarely will you regret having kept your temper. Whereas venting anger breeds more anger, restraining anger often cools the fires of conflict. It can even promote your value and character in the eyes of those observing you.

PROMISE FROM GOD Psalm 103:8 *The Lord is merciful and gracious; he is slow to get angry and full of unfailing love.*

ANXIETY

See **WORRY**

APPEARANCE

How much does appearance matter?
1 Samuel 16:7 *But the Lord said to Samuel, "Don't judge by his appearance or height, for I have rejected him. The Lord doesn't make decisions the way you do! People judge by outward appearance, but the Lord looks at a person's thoughts and intentions."*
The Lord values the inner person of faith, character, and integrity. Likewise, leaders should be neither preoccupied nor deceived by image and outward

impressions of themselves or others. Appropriate attention is given to appearance, but never at the cost of devaluing the inner person.

What is the danger in basing my evaluations on appearances?

2 Corinthians 11:13-15 *These people are false apostles. They have fooled you by disguising themselves as apostles of Christ. But I am not surprised! Even Satan can disguise himself as an angel of light. So it is no wonder his servants can also do it by pretending to be godly ministers.*

Matthew 23:28 *You try to look like upright people outwardly, but inside your hearts are filled with hypocrisy and lawlessness.*

Appearances can cover up people's true intentions. Leaders should focus on substance, not allowing themselves to be seduced by image. Even religious activity that appears to be good can be a cover for self-centered interests.

How can I see beyond appearances?

Matthew 7:16-21 *You can detect them by the way they act, just as you can identify a tree by its fruit. . . . A healthy tree produces good fruit, and an unhealthy tree produces bad fruit. . . . Yes, the way to identify a tree or a person is by the kind of fruit that is produced. Not all people who sound religious are really godly.*

1 John 4:1 *Dear friends, do not believe everyone who claims to speak by the Spirit. You must test them to see if the spirit they have comes from God. For there are many false prophets in the world.*

Leaders must be "fruit inspectors," looking beyond appearances and words to the actual behavior and character of people. In matters of faith and spirituality, orthodox theology is an essential test of authentic faith in Jesus Christ. Good works alone are not sufficient. There must be an essential congruence between words and works, faith and life, character and conduct.

How important is it for leaders to maintain a good appearance?

1 Corinthians 6:19-20 *Or don't you know that your body is the temple of the Holy Spirit, who lives in you and was given to you by God? You do not belong to yourself, for God bought you with a high price. So you must honor God with your body.*

While appearance is not primary, it is still a significant element in your interaction with others. As you walk with Christ, people will watch to see if your faith is genuine. As temples of the Holy Spirit, you are to honor God through your body in every way, through sexual purity as well as personal care for your health and appearance.

PROMISE FROM GOD Colossians 3:17 *And whatever you do or say, let it be as a representative of the Lord Jesus, all the while giving thanks through him to God the Father.*

APPROVAL

See also **ACCEPT/ACCEPTANCE, CRITICISM**

Where do leaders look for approval?

Galatians 2:19 *When I tried to keep the law, I realized I could never earn God's approval.*

Romans 8:1-2, 15-17 *So now there is no condemnation for those who belong to Christ Jesus. For the power of the life-giving Spirit has freed you through Christ Jesus from the power of sin that leads to death. . . . So you should not be like cowering, fearful slaves. You should behave instead like God's very own children, adopted into his family—calling him "Father, dear Father." For his Holy Spirit speaks to us deep in our hearts and tells us that we are God's children. And since we are his children, we will share his treasures—for everything God gives to his Son, Christ, is ours, too.*

No one—not even leaders—can earn God's approval; instead, God freely gives his approval through people's faith in Jesus Christ. You are God's beloved child, adopted into his family by grace. You have been approved because of what Jesus did for you.

Luke 10:17-20 *When the seventy-two disciples returned, they joyfully reported to him, "Lord, even the demons obey us when we use your name!" "Yes," he told them, "I saw Satan falling from heaven as a flash of lightning! And I have given you authority over all the power of the enemy, and you can walk among snakes and scorpions and crush them. Nothing will injure you. But don't rejoice just because evil spirits obey you; rejoice because your names are registered as citizens of heaven."*

Your approval is based on personal faith in Jesus Christ, not on your performance. Your performance matters (see Matthew 25:23 below and Ephesians 2:10), but it is the expression of gratitude for your approval, not the basis for it. You may be privileged to do amazing works in Jesus' name, but never lose sight that your identity is rooted in God's grace, not the works he allows you to do.

Matthew 25:23 *The master said, "Well done, my good and faithful servant. You have been faithful in handling this small amount, so now I will give you many*

more responsibilities. Let's celebrate together!"
While people's ultimate approval is rooted in grace, God has entrusted the stewardship of his creation and the ongoing ministry of Christ into our care. He expects those to whom he has entrusted leadership to be faithful in the work and service he has given them to do. Faithfulness will be rewarded with his holy commendation and an even greater participation in his work.

What brings the Lord's approval?

Proverbs 12:2 *The Lord approves of those who are good, but he condemns those who plan wickedness.*

Romans 2:13 *For it is not merely knowing the law that brings God's approval. Those who obey the law will be declared right in God's sight.*
Faith in God and obedience to his Word bring approval from him.

How should I respond when others disapprove of my faith?

Psalm 27:1 *The Lord is my light and my salvation—so why should I be afraid? The Lord protects me from danger—so why should I tremble?*
Your value is determined by God's decision, not by the decision or derision of others. The exhortation to live for an audience of One reminds you that your ultimate purpose is to please the God who made you and redeemed you, no matter what others may think of you.

John 5:41 *Your approval or disapproval means nothing to me.*
Jesus' strong words came from his unwavering confidence in God's approval and his own freedom from human opinion. You, too, can live free from the bondage of human opinion and criticism by knowing God's love and approval more and more fully.

How can I communicate approval to others?
Philippians 1:3-6 *Every time I think of you, I give thanks to my God. I always pray for you, and I make my requests with a heart full of joy because you have been my partners in spreading the Good News about Christ from the time you first heard it until now. And I am sure that God, who began the good work within you, will continue his work until it is finally finished on that day when Christ Jesus comes back again.*

2 Thessalonians 1:3-4 *Dear brothers and sisters, we always thank God for you, as is right, for we are thankful that your faith is flourishing and you are all growing in love for each other. We proudly tell God's other churches about your endurance and faithfulness in all the persecutions and hardships you are suffering.*
Paul's letters were filled with expressions of approval and encouragement. Leaders are often in the place of pointing out what is wrong or what can be better. Never forget to build on the foundation of approval that is built on people's worth in Christ.

PROMISES FROM GOD Numbers 6:24-26 *May the Lord bless you and protect you. May the Lord smile on you and be gracious to you. May the Lord show you his favor and give you his peace.*

Romans 15:7 *So accept each other just as Christ has accepted you; then God will be glorified.*

ASSERTIVENESS

What basis does a leader have for being assertive?
Matthew 23:23-24 *How terrible it will be for you teachers of religious law and you Pharisees. Hypocrites! For*

you are careful to tithe even the tiniest part of your income, but you ignore the important things of the law—justice, mercy, and faith. You should tithe, yes, but you should not leave undone the more important things. Blind guides! You strain your water so you won't accidentally swallow a gnat; then you swallow a camel!

Jesus was often assertive in his relationship with the religious leaders of his day. Assertiveness means standing up for right or making known your legitimate needs, concerns, and differences. Leaders must be assertive. There are times when you may be tempted to be quiet or look the other way when others are making unethical choices or behaving in inappropriate ways. But you must stand up for what you believe and confront others when necessary. Assertiveness, however, must be as loving as it is bold.

How should I exercise assertiveness with others?

1 Corinthians 4:14 *I am not writing these things to shame you, but to warn you as my beloved children.*

Paul was assertive in addressing a number of problems in Corinth. His assertiveness was rooted in his love and relationship with the people as well as his sense of accountability before the Lord.

What are the consequences for failing to be assertive?

Ezekiel 3:17-21 *Whenever you receive a message from me, pass it on to the people immediately. If I warn the wicked, saying, "You are under the penalty of death," but you fail to deliver the warning, they will die in their sins. And I will hold you responsible. . . . But if you warn them and they repent, they will live, and you will have saved your own life, too.*

Leaders are watch keepers over the people they serve by looking out for their welfare. Not every leader has the level of spiritual responsibility God assigned to Ezekiel, but we are all called to uphold biblical standards as appropriate in our relationships and responsibilities. You must have the courage to tell people the bad news so that they can respond to the good news of God's grace.

PROMISE FROM GOD 1 John 2:28 *And now, dear children, continue to live in fellowship with Christ so that when he returns, you will be full of courage and not shrink back from him in shame.*

ATTITUDE

What kind of attitude does God want leaders to have toward others?

Philippians 2:5, 7 *Your attitude should be the same that Christ Jesus had. . . . He made himself nothing; he took the humble position of a slave.*

Jesus, the ultimate Leader was also the ultimate Servant. Leaders should maintain a servant attitude as they take responsibility for keeping the purpose before the group and for providing the resources and direction they need to fulfill the task before them.

What kind of attitude should mark a leader's outlook on life?

Philippians 4:4-6 *Always be full of joy in the Lord. I say it again—rejoice! . . . Don't worry about anything; instead, pray about everything. Tell God what you need, and thank him for all he has done.*

1 Thessalonians 5:16-18 *Always be joyful. Keep on praying. No matter what happens, always be thankful, for this is God's will for you who belong to Christ Jesus.*

Leaders, who often know all about the things that are wrong with a situation, nevertheless know that one thing is always right: the Lord who loves us is there at all times, in all places. That's why leaders are called to cultivate a holy confidence in God that lightens every load and brightens every circumstance.

What are the practical benefits of a faith-filled attitude?

Proverbs 17:22 *A cheerful heart is good medicine, but a broken spirit saps a person's strength.*

Proverbs 14:30 *A relaxed attitude lengthens life; jealousy rots it away.*

Philippians 4:11-13 *For I have learned how to get along happily whether I have much or little. I know how to live on almost nothing or with everything. I have learned the secret of living in every situation, whether it is with a full stomach or empty, with plenty or little. For I can do everything with the help of Christ who gives me the strength I need.*

2 Corinthians 12:9-10 *Each time he said, "My gracious favor is all you need. My power works best in your weakness." So now I am glad to boast about my weaknesses, so that the power of Christ may work through me. Since I know it is all for Christ's good, I am quite content with my weaknesses and with insults, hardships, persecutions, and calamities. For when I am weak, then I am strong.*

Attitude changes everything. Faith enables you to base your attitude on the character of God, not on the circumstances of life. You can even see that weakness and struggle are the raw materials for God's mighty works.

What attitudes please God?

Romans 14:17-19 *For the Kingdom of God is not a matter of what we eat or drink, but of living a life of goodness and peace and joy in the Holy Spirit. If you serve Christ with this attitude, you will please God. And other people will approve of you, too. So then, let us aim for harmony in the church and try to build each other up.*

Romans 15:5-6 *May God, who gives this patience and encouragement, help you live in complete harmony with each other—each with the attitude of Christ Jesus toward the other. Then all of you can join together with one voice, giving praise and glory to God, the Father of our Lord Jesus Christ.*

God is pleased with a peace-making attitude that puts the welfare of the believing community ahead of your own preferences. You should desire to contribute to a holy harmony in all your relationships.

Ephesians 4:21-24 *Since you have heard all about him and have learned the truth that is in Jesus, throw off your old evil nature and your former way of life, which is rotten through and through, full of lust and deception. Instead, there must be a spiritual renewal of your thoughts and attitudes. You must display a new nature because you are a new person, created in God's likeness—righteous, holy, and true.*

God is pleased with a humble attitude that is willing to be changed from the inside out, starting with your thoughts and attitudes. With his help, you can actually both think yourself into a new way of living and live yourself into a new way thinking. What's most important is that you not yield to your sinful nature which makes you want to go back to the old way of living that was harmful to you.

1 Peter 4:1-2 *So then, since Christ suffered physical pain, you must arm yourselves with the same attitude he had, and be ready to suffer, too. For if you are willing to*

suffer for Christ, you have decided to stop sinning. And you won't spend the rest of your life chasing after evil desires, but you will be anxious to do the will of God.
God is pleased with a self-sacrificing attitude that is willing to suffer for the sake of others. This suffering may come from longer hours, the heavy burden of hard decisions, doing the right-but-unpopular thing, or knowing information about people and circumstances that you wish you didn't know. A humble spirit that accepts the hard things honors God.

PROMISES FROM GOD Matthew 5:3-8 *God blesses those who realize their need for him, for the Kingdom of Heaven is given to them. . . . God blesses those who are gentle and lowly, for the whole earth will belong to them. . . . God blesses those whose hearts are pure, for they will see God.*

AUTHORITY

See also **POWER, SERVANTHOOD**

Why is human authority necessary?
Judges 21:25 *In those days Israel had no king, so the people did whatever seemed right in their own eyes.*

1 Peter 2:13-14 *For the Lord's sake, accept all authority—the king as head of state, and the officials he has appointed. For the king has sent them to punish all who do wrong and to honor those who do right.*
God has appointed human authorities to bring order and security in society. It is the same in business, the church, and the family. Authority properly exercised gives the people involved security and order.

Where does a leader's authority come from?
Proverbs 21:1 *The king's heart is like a stream of water directed by the Lord; he turns it wherever he pleases.*

Romans 13:1-2 *Obey the government, for God is the one who put it there. All governments have been placed in power by God. So those who refuse to obey the laws of the land are refusing to obey God, and punishment will follow.* God wants us to obey the authorities because they have been appointed to govern our lives. Unless they order us to denounce God or directly disobey his commands as found in the Bible, we should submit to them, even if we don't like what they are demanding.

Matthew 28:18-19 *Jesus came and told his disciples, "I have been given complete authority in heaven and on earth. Therefore, go and make disciples of all the nations."*

John 19:11 *Jesus said, "You would have no power over me at all unless it were given to you from above."* All authority comes from God and is given for the sake of fulfilling responsibility and contributing to the welfare of God's people and creation. Power is not given for its own sake, but for the sake of getting the right things done well. Leaders will answer to the Lord for how they steward the power and authority that have been entrusted to them.

How should I use my authority as a leader?
Philippians 2:3-7 *Don't be selfish; don't live to make a good impression on others. Be humble, thinking of others as better than yourself. Don't think only about your own affairs, but be interested in others, too, and what they are doing. Your attitude should be the same that Christ Jesus had. Though he was God, he did not demand and cling to his rights as God. He made himself nothing; he took*

the humble position of a slave and appeared in human form.
Use your authority for the sake of serving others. Leadership is for service.

Matthew 8:8-10 *Then the officer said, "Lord, I am not worthy to have you come into my home. Just say the word from where you are, and my servant will be healed! I know, because I am under the authority of my superior officers and I have authority over my soldiers. I only need to say, 'Go,' and they go, or 'Come,' and they come. And if I say to my slaves, 'Do this or that,' they do it." When Jesus heard this, he was amazed. Turning to the crowd, he said, "I tell you the truth, I haven't seen faith like this in all the land of Israel!"*
The officer displayed humility and faith in his understanding of authority. He knew both the power and the limitations of his authority. He did not presume that because he held a position of authority in the military that he could order the Lord around. He humbled himself for the sake of helping his own servant. This kind of leadership will succeed because it does not coerce compliance, but instead wins commitment.

How can I exercise my authority without feeling reticent or intimidated?
Matthew 10:1 *Jesus called his twelve disciples to him and gave them authority to cast out evil spirits and to heal every kind of disease and illness.*

2 Timothy 1:6-7 *This is why I remind you to fan into flames the spiritual gift God gave you when I laid my hands on you. For God has not given us a spirit of fear and timidity, but of power, love, and self-discipline.*

1 Timothy 4:11-12 *Teach these things and insist that everyone learn them. Don't let anyone think less of you*

because you are young. Be an example to all believers in what you teach, in the way you live, in your love, your faith, and your purity.
As leaders, we have been delegated our authority by Christ. Therefore, use your authority in Christ without being intimidated by spiritual powers, social customs, age, or any other factor.

PROMISE FROM GOD John 17:2 *You have given him authority over everyone in all the earth. He gives eternal life to each one you have given him.*

BALANCE

See also **BURNOUT, SPIRITUAL DISCIPLINES, STRESS, TIME**

What is balance?
Matthew 22:37-40 *Jesus replied, "'You must love the Lord your God with all your heart, all your soul, and all your mind.' This is the first and greatest commandment. A second is equally important: 'Love your neighbor as yourself.' All the other commandments and all the demands of the prophets are based on these two commandments."*

Ecclesiastes 3:1 *There is a time for everything, a season for every activity under heaven.*

John 17:4-5 *I brought glory to you here on earth by doing everything you told me to do. And now, Father, bring me into the glory we shared before the world began.*
Balance means living a life that honors God, others, and yourself in the way you use your gifts and spend your time and resources. One of the greatest mistakes leaders make is getting out of balance by over-empha-

sizing one aspect of their responsibilities at the cost of other areas. God assures you that there is a time for everything as well as time for everything he calls you to do. Jesus, with all his potential and all the needs around him, left much undone yet completed all God had given him to do.

How can I, as a leader, bring balance into my life?

Mark 1:35-38 *The next morning Jesus awoke long before daybreak and went out alone into the wilderness to pray. Later Simon and the others went out to find him. They said, "Everyone is asking for you." But he replied, "We must go on to other towns as well, and I will preach to them, too, because that is why I came."*

Luke 5:16 *But Jesus often withdrew to the wilderness for prayer.*

Jesus modeled a life balanced by involvement and withdrawal, action and reflection, mission and meditation, effort and then time for spiritual energizing. This pace allowed him to remain open to God's direction instead of human pressures. Balance helps you realize that the need and even the opportunity are not necessarily the call of God.

PROMISES FROM GOD Titus 2:12 *And we are instructed to turn from godless living and sinful pleasures. We should live in this evil world with self-control, right conduct, and devotion to God.*

Psalm 119:5-7 *Oh, that my actions would consistently reflect your principles! Then I will not be disgraced when I compare my life with your commands. When I learn your righteous laws, I will thank you by living as I should.*

BETRAYAL

See also **CONFLICT, FORGIVENESS**

What can go wrong in a leader's relationships?

2 Samuel 15:9-10 *Absalom went to Hebron. But while he was there, he sent secret messengers to every part of Israel to stir up a rebellion against the king.*

Psalm 55:20-21 *As for this friend of mine, he betrayed me; he broke his promises. His words are as smooth as cream, but in his heart is war. His words are as soothing as lotion, but underneath are daggers!*

Matthew 26:20-21 *When it was evening, Jesus sat down at the table with the twelve disciples. While they were eating, he said, "The truth is, one of you will betray me."*

2 Timothy 4:10 *Demas has deserted me because he loves the things of this life and has gone to Thessalonica.*
Betrayal is one of the saddest realities of leadership. David was betrayed by his son Absalom. Jesus was betrayed by Judas, and Paul was betrayed by Demas.

How should I treat those who betray me?

1 Samuel 23:12-13 *Again David asked, "Will these men of Keilah really betray me and my men to Saul?" And the Lord replied, "Yes, they will betray you." So David and his men—about six hundred of them now—left Keilah and began roaming the countryside.*
Though David had protected the town of Keilah from the Philistines, the people of Keilah would not give David protection from Saul. You cannot expect people to reciprocate for the support or kindness you show. Follow God's direction (see 1 Samuel 23:4) and leave your cause in God's hands.

John 13:2-5 *It was time for supper, and the Devil had already enticed Judas, son of Simon Iscariot, to carry out his plan to betray Jesus. Jesus knew that the Father had given him authority over everything and that he had come from God and would return to God. So he got up from the table, took off his robe, wrapped a towel around his waist, and poured water into a basin. Then he began to wash the disciples' feet and to wipe them with the towel he had around him.*

Jesus loved his disciples, including Judas, to the very end. His love was based on God's love for him, not their faithfulness—or lack thereof. Leaders must be aware of the tendency to "use" those they lead to help themselves feel loved, special, or important. Realize that people will fail you at times, so look to God for your ultimate affirmation and satisfaction.

PROMISES FROM GOD Romans 3:3 *True, some of them were unfaithful; but just because they broke their promises, does that mean God will break his promises?*

Isaiah 54:10 *"For the mountains may depart and the hills disappear, but even then I will remain loyal to you. My covenant of blessing will never be broken," says the Lord, who has mercy on you.*

BIBLE

Why should leaders keep God's Word before them daily?

Deuteronomy 17:18-20 *When he sits on the throne as king, he must copy these laws on a scroll. . . . He must always keep this copy of the law with him and read it daily as long as he lives. That way he will learn to fear the Lord his God by obeying all the terms of this law. This regular reading will prevent him from becoming proud and acting as if he is above his fellow citizens. It will also prevent him from turning away from these commands in the smallest way.*

The Bible gives leaders more than practical wisdom. God's Word shapes their hearts, minds and souls. It helps leaders keep their focus on God's honor. It keeps them humble alongside others. Obedience to God's Word ensures an enduring legacy.

What are the benefits of leading according to God's Word?

Psalm 1:1-2 *Oh, the joys of those who do not follow the advice of the wicked, or stand around with sinners, or join in with scoffers. But they delight in doing everything the Lord wants; day and night they think about his law.*

Meditation on God's Word exposes the foolishness of worldly wisdom. It provides the basis for your decision making, your strategy, your conduct, and your interaction with others.

How can I use God's Word in the lives of those I lead?

2 Timothy 3:16-17 *All Scripture is inspired by God and is useful to teach us what is true and to make us realize what is wrong in our lives. It straightens us out and teaches us to do what is right. It is God's way of preparing us in every way, fully equipped for every good thing God wants us to do.*

Scripture not only shapes leaders, but also gives leaders the method for shaping the lives of those they lead. God's Word shows the path for your spiritual journey (doctrine that is true), reveals how you sin and stray (disclosure of your need), gives godly rebuke to return you to the way (discipline to correct you), and teaches you how to live in the power of the Spirit (discipleship) for remaining faithful. If you intentionally teach, disclose, discipline, and disciple with clear direction from God's Word, those you lead will be served in the most effective, productive way.

PROMISE FROM GOD Hebrews 8:10 *I will put my laws in their minds so they will understand them, and I will write them on their hearts so they will obey them.*

BITTERNESS

See **BETRAYAL, FORGIVENESS**

BLAME

See **FORGIVENESS, RESPONSIBILITY**

BLESSINGS

What is the danger inherent in God's blessings in leaders' lives?

Deuteronomy 8:14-18 *Do not become proud . . . and forget the Lord your God, who rescued you. . . . He did it so you would never think that it was your own strength and energy that made you wealthy. Always remember that it is the Lord your God who gives you power.*

There are no self-made people. In the midst of great blessings remember the source of those blessings.

How should I respond to my blessings?

1 Corinthians 3:6-9 *My job was to plant the seed in your hearts, and Apollos watered it, but it was God, not we, who made it grow. The ones who do the planting or*

watering aren't important, but God is important because he is the one who makes the seed grow. . . . We work together as partners who belong to God.
Leaders often enjoy the fruit of a work well done by the team. They are also in a position to experience negative consequences where they have not led well. Therefore, hold blessings loosely. Do not be motivated by them, but be grateful for whatever God gives.

How can I bless those I lead?
Matthew 25:21 *The master was full of praise. "Well done, my good and faithful servant. You have been faithful in handling this small amount, so now I will give you many more responsibilities. Let's celebrate together!"*
The leader's role is to say thank you and to bless the people in the group or organization. Withholding praise or well-deserved remuneration cheats people and hurts all involved. Praise and affirmation, properly given, will enlarge people's hearts and deepen their commitment to you and to God.

PROMISE FROM GOD Galatians 6:9 *So don't get tired of doing what is good. Don't get discouraged and give up, for we will reap a harvest of blessing at the appropriate time.*

BROKENNESS

See also **VULNERABILITY, WEAKNESSES**

Why is brokenness an important attitude for leaders to develop?
Psalm 34:18 *The Lord is close to the brokenhearted; he rescues those who are crushed in spirit.*
Brokenness is the awareness of your full dependence

on God. It signifies the breaking of your pride and self-sufficiency.

How will an attitude of brokenness affect me?

Psalm 51:17 *The sacrifice you want is a broken spirit. A broken and repentant heart, O God, you will not despise.*
You will draw closer to God when brokenness over your sin makes you open to God's grace.

Psalm 147:3 *He heals the brokenhearted, binding up their wounds.*
When you turn to God in brokenness over your sin, he begins to heal you and restore you.

Job 2:8-10 *Job scraped his skin with a piece of broken pottery as he sat among the ashes. His wife said to him, "Are you still trying to maintain your integrity? Curse God and die." But Job replied, "You talk like a godless woman. Should we accept only good things from the hand of God and never anything bad?" So in all this, Job said nothing wrong.*
The alternative to brokenness before God is bitterness. Like Job, you can better resist bitterness in your immediate circumstances when you keep your focus on God and the larger picture.

Job 42:5-6 *I had heard about you before, but now I have seen you with my own eyes. I take back everything I said, and I sit in dust and ashes to show my repentance.*
Brokenness comes as you more clearly realize God's holiness in contrast to your own sinfulness.

How should I respond to brokenness?

Psalm 51:1-4 *Have mercy on me, O God, because of your unfailing love. Because of your great compassion, blot out the stain of my sins. Wash me clean from my guilt.*

Purify me from my sin. For I recognize my shameful deeds—they haunt me day and night. Against you, and you alone, have I sinned; I have done what is evil in your sight. You will be proved right in what you say, and your judgment against me is just.
When you fall, you must also fall to your knees to be restored. David was guilty of adultery and murder. Yet when confronted (see 2 Samuel 12), David didn't run from God, make excuses for his failure, or give up in despair. Instead, he acknowledged God's justice and cast himself on God's mercy.

John 21:15 *After breakfast Jesus said to Simon Peter, "Simon son of John, do you love me more than these?" "Yes, Lord," Peter replied, "you know I love you."*
When others fall, come alongside them. It has been said that despair is a greater sin than any that would cause it. Peter's denial of Jesus had broken his spirit. But Jesus, in this resurrection appearance, restored Peter. He gave Peter the opportunity to "unsay" his denials by reaffirming his love. Be there to help, and allow the Lord to work his miracle of restoration.

PROMISE FROM GOD Psalm 34:18 *The Lord is close to the brokenhearted; he rescues those who are crushed in spirit.*

BURNOUT

See also **BALANCE, SABBATH, STRESS**

How do I know if I am experiencing burnout?
2 Samuel 21:15 *When David and his men were in the thick of battle, David became weak and exhausted.*

Psalm 38:8 *I am exhausted and completely crushed. My groans come from an anguished heart.*
If you become weak and exhausted in the middle of doing your work, you may be experiencing burnout.

1 Kings 19:14 *I alone am left, and now they are trying to kill me, too.*
If you despair because your work seems fruitless, you may be experiencing burnout.

Psalm 69:1-2 *The floodwaters are up to my neck. Deeper and deeper I sink into the mire; I can't find a foothold to stand on.*
If you feel overwhelmed by everything that is going on in your life, you may be experiencing burnout.

Jeremiah 45:3 *You have said, "I am overwhelmed with trouble! Haven't I had enough pain already? And now the Lord has added more!"*
If you feel bitter toward God, you may be experiencing burnout.

Why are leaders in danger of burning out?
2 Corinthians 4:7 *But this precious treasure—this light and power that now shine within us—is held in perishable containers, that is, in our weak bodies. So everyone can see that our glorious power is from God and is not our own.*
Leaders are human. They get tired, frustrated, discouraged, and confused. They also fail and sin time and again. Yet, by God's grace, your humanity does not disqualify you from serving God in all that you do. In fact, it becomes the means for God to reveal his power and mercy to you and through you.

What can I do when I sense that I may be burning out?
Isaiah 40:28-31 *Don't you know that the Lord is*

the everlasting God, the Creator of all the earth? He never grows faint or weary. No one can measure the depths of his understanding. He gives power to those who are tired and worn out; he offers strength to the weak. Even youths will become exhausted, and young men will give up. But those who wait on the Lord will find new strength. They will fly high on wings like eagles. They will run and not grow weary. They will walk and not faint.

Much of your weariness may be arising from impatience and anxious striving. A key to renewal and refreshment is waiting on the Lord. Waiting does not mean inactivity, but rather living with a calm reliance on God's provision and God's timing. Waiting means faith, not force.

Matthew 11:28-30 *Then Jesus said, "Come to me, all of you who are weary and carry heavy burdens, and I will give you rest. Take my yoke upon you. Let me teach you, because I am humble and gentle, and you will find rest for your souls. For my yoke fits perfectly, and the burden I give you is light."*

You may sometimes find it difficult to rest. At times, leaders mistakenly believe that productivity requires constant activity. God graciously invites you to unburden yourself and rest in him.

Exodus 18:21-23 *Find some capable, honest men. . . . They will help you carry the load, making the task easier for you. If you follow this advice, . . . then you will be able to endure the pressures.*

Sometimes you might be able to delegate some of your workload.

Exodus 23:12 *Work for six days, and rest on the seventh.*

Regular, consistent rest is an important part of avoiding and recovering from burnout.

How does Jesus view my struggles with pressure and burnout?

Hebrews 4:15-16 *This High Priest of ours understands our weaknesses, for he faced all of the same temptations we do, yet he did not sin. So let us come boldly to the throne of our gracious God. There we will receive his mercy, and we will find grace to help us when we need it.*
You can rely on the Lord's merciful understanding and his holy empathy with your humanity. Instead of condemnation you find mercy; instead of criticism you get comfort and encouragement.

PROMISES FROM GOD Psalm 23:1-3 *The Lord is my shepherd; I have everything I need. He lets me rest in green meadows; he leads me beside peaceful streams. He renews my strength. He guides me along right paths, bringing honor to his name.*

BUSINESS

See also **CALL OF GOD/CALLING, WORK**

Is God interested in my success in business?

Proverbs 31:16 *She goes out to inspect a field and buys it; with her earnings she plants a vineyard.*
God thinks highly of people who are enterprising and hardworking.

Acts 18:2-3 *A Jew named Aquila . . . had recently arrived from Italy with his wife, Priscilla. . . . Paul lived and worked with them, for they were tentmakers just as he was.*
Aquila and Priscilla were Christian leaders in ministry and in business. They are examples of early Christians

who used their successful business to serve God.

Ephesians 6:6-7 *Work hard. . . . As slaves of Christ, do the will of God with all your heart. Work with enthusiasm, as though you were working for the Lord rather than for people.*
How you do what you do reveals the nature of your commitment to Christ. Hard work done with excellence and integrity honors God and may bring material resources that can be further used for God's glory.

What principles should guide how I conduct my business?

Leviticus 19:13 *Do not cheat or rob anyone. Always pay your hired workers promptly.*
You should be fair and responsive to your employees.

Proverbs 24:27 *Develop your business first before building your house.*
Understand your responsibility to provide a solid foundation for life. Focus on establishing your business before you overcommit to comfort at home.

Proverbs 16:11 *The Lord demands fairness in every business deal; he sets the standard.*
Integrity is an essential mark of Christian leaders. Anything less dishonors the Lord, those you lead, and those you serve.

Ecclesiastes 9:10 *Whatever you do, do well.*
Pursue excellence.

Deuteronomy 25:15-16 *Yes, use honest weights and measures, so that you will enjoy a long life in the land the Lord your God is giving you. Those who cheat with dishonest weights and measures are detestable to the Lord your God.*

Ezekiel 22:12 *There are hired murderers, loan racketeers, and extortioners everywhere! They never even think of me and my commands, says the Sovereign Lord.*
Be honest. God condemns dishonest and violent means to become successful.

Ruth 4:2 *Boaz called ten leaders from the town and asked them to sit as witnesses.*
Like Boaz, always conduct your business above board and in public, with no hidden kickbacks or shady deals.

Psalm 112:5 *All goes well for those who are generous, who lend freely and conduct their business fairly.*
It is important to be generous in your business dealings—it is an investment that will certainly come back to you later!

Amos 8:4-5 *Listen to this, you who rob the poor and trample the needy! You can't wait for the Sabbath day to be over and the religious festivals to end so you can get back to cheating the helpless.*
Serving God through your business during the week means that you live in harmony with what you profess on Sundays.

Mark 12:17 *"Well, then," Jesus said, "give to Caesar what belongs to him. But everything that belongs to God must be given to God."*
Always be sure to pay all of your taxes.

Luke 14:28 *Don't begin until you count the cost.*
Whenever you start a project or a business venture, plan ahead and make sure that you can carry it through.

James 4:13-15 *Look here, you people who say, "Today or tomorrow we are going to a certain town and will*

stay there a year. We will do business there and make a profit." How do you know what will happen tomorrow? For your life is like the morning fog—it's here a little while, then it's gone. What you ought to say is, "If the Lord wants us to, we will live and do this or that."
Whatever business ventures you pursue, remember that God is your Lord and that you are completely dependent on him in everything.

PROMISE FROM GOD Psalm 37:37 *Look at those who are honest and good, for a wonderful future lies before those who love peace.*

CALL OF GOD/CALLING

See also **BUSINESS, GOD'S WILL, WORK**

How can I know God's calling for my life?
Jeremiah 1:4-5 *The Lord gave me a message. . . . I knew you before I formed you in your mother's womb. Before you were born I set you apart and appointed you as my spokesman to the world.*
Sometimes God may call you to fulfill a very specific ministry. When that happens, God will make sure that you know it.

1 Corinthians 12:4-7 *There are different kinds of spiritual gifts, but it is the same Holy Spirit who is the source of them all. . . . A spiritual gift is given to each of us as a means of helping the entire church.*

2 Timothy 4:5 *Complete the ministry God has given you.*
God has given each of us a special ministry that he wants us to perform in the church to build up the body

and bring glory to his name. You have been gifted in a special way to meet a special need right where you are.

1 Corinthians 7:17 *You must accept whatever situation the Lord has put you in, and continue on as you were when God first called you.*
Paul explains that the call to follow Jesus does not necessarily mean that you will have to change jobs. In fact, he encourages people to stay in their current positions, focusing on obedience to God in them. You may need to stay right where you are, serving God in whatever capacity you now fulfill.

How can I know what my calling is?
Psalm 119:105 *Your word is a lamp for my feet and a light for my path.*
The first step in knowing your calling is to get to know God intimately through his Word and let him guide you.

Daniel 1:17 *God gave these four young men an unusual aptitude for learning the literature and science of the time.*
God has given each of us special aptitudes and abilities. A second step to knowing your calling is seeing the kinds of desires and abilities God has given you.

Acts 20:24 *My life is worth nothing unless I use it for doing the work assigned me by the Lord Jesus.*
When God gives you a specific calling, it fills your thoughts and energies so that you pursue it wholeheartedly.

Romans 12:2 *Let God transform you into a new person by changing the way you think. Then you will know what God wants you to do.*
When you let God transform you by the power of his Holy Spirit, he will show you what he wants you to do.

PROMISE FROM GOD 1 Thessalonians 5:23-24 *May the God of peace make you holy in every way, and may your whole spirit and soul and body be kept blameless until that day when our Lord Jesus Christ comes again. God, who calls you, is faithful; he will do this.*

CARING

How do I care for those I lead?

1 Samuel 30:21-24 *When they reached Besor Brook and met the two hundred men who had been too tired to go with them, David greeted them joyfully. But some troublemakers among David's men said, "They didn't go with us, so they can't have any of the plunder. . . ." But David said, "No, my brothers! Don't be selfish with what the Lord has given us. He has kept us safe and helped us defeat the enemy. . . . We share and share alike—those who go to battle and those who guard the equipment."*

Leadership keeps the people in mind, not just their productivity. You may at times have to compromise and accommodate for the reality of human struggles and trials.

1 Thessalonians 1:2-3 *We always thank God for all of you and pray for you constantly. As we talk to our God and Father about you, we think of your faithful work, your loving deeds, and your continual anticipation of the return of our Lord Jesus Christ.*

You can affirm and pray for those you lead.

PROMISE FROM GOD 1 Peter 5:7 *Give all your worries and cares to God, for he cares about what happens to you.*

CHALLENGES

How do challenges shape my life as a leader?

Romans 15:20 *My ambition has always been to preach the Good News where the name of Christ has never been heard, rather than where a church has already been started by someone else.*

Leaders are not satisfied with the status quo. You should want to follow God's leading into uncharted waters. Paul's vision to preach the gospel in new places continually drove him to new challenges.

2 Corinthians 4:11 *Yes, we live under constant danger of death because we serve Jesus, so that the life of Jesus will be obvious in our dying bodies.*

2 Corinthians 11:26 *I have traveled many weary miles. I have faced danger from flooded rivers and from robbers. I have faced danger from my own people, the Jews, as well as from the Gentiles. I have faced danger in the cities, in the deserts, and on the stormy seas. And I have faced danger from men who claim to be Christians but are not.*

Facing dangers of various sorts is part of the challenge of serving God in all things. These challenges reveal God's grace and power, as well as teaching you to develop endurance as well as the gifts God has given you.

How do I find strength to face my challenges?

1 Samuel 17:41-47 *Goliath walked out toward David with his shield bearer ahead of him, sneering in contempt at this ruddy-faced boy. . . . David shouted in reply, "You come to me with sword, spear, and javelin, but I come to you in the name of the Lord Almighty—the God of the armies of Israel, whom you have defied. Today the Lord*

will conquer you. . . . And everyone will know that the Lord does not need weapons to rescue his people. It is his battle, not ours."
David kept his eyes on God's promise instead of on his opponent's power. You must maintain faith when others are intimidated by the challenges.

1 Chronicles 28:20 *Then David continued, "Be strong and courageous, and do the work. Don't be afraid or discouraged by the size of the task, for the Lord God, my God, is with you. He will not fail you or forsake you."*

2 Samuel 22:30 *In your strength I can crush an army; with my God I can scale any wall.*
When God calls, God provides. Do not focus on the size of the task, but on the size of your God who will never fail.

Joshua 1:7, 9 *Be strong and very courageous. Obey all the laws Moses gave you. Do not turn away from them, and you will be successful in everything you do. . . . I command you—be strong and courageous! Do not be afraid or discouraged. For the Lord your God is with you wherever you go.*

Psalm 37:5 *Commit everything you do to the Lord. Trust him, and he will help you.*

1 Corinthians 16:13 *Be on guard. Stand true to what you believe. Be courageous. Be strong.*
Leaders encourage themselves and others to be strong because of Christ's power within them. Maintain your hope in God's promises and power.

What do I need to know about challenges and risks?
Ecclesiastes 10:9 *When you work in a quarry, stones might fall and crush you! When you chop wood,*

there is danger with each stroke of your ax! Such are the risks of life.

Proverbs 14:16 *The wise are cautious and avoid danger; fools plunge ahead with great confidence.*

Proverbs 22:3 *A prudent person foresees the danger ahead and takes precautions; the simpleton goes blindly on and suffers the consequences.*

Romans 8:35 *Can anything ever separate us from Christ's love? Does it mean he no longer loves us if we have trouble or calamity, or are persecuted, or are hungry or cold or in danger or threatened with death?*

Leaders understand that growth and success occur at the edge of risk. This does not excuse taking foolish chances, but it does mean that you can call upon God when you are put in a hard place. Whatever the degree of risk, you trust in God and his love for you.

PROMISE FROM GOD Ephesians 6:10-11 *A final word: Be strong with the Lord's mighty power. Put on all of God's armor so that you will be able to stand firm against all strategies and tricks of the Devil.*

CHANGE

How do I manage change?

Acts 10:45-48 *The Jewish believers who came with Peter were amazed that the gift of the Holy Spirit had been poured out upon the Gentiles, too. And there could be no doubt about it, for they heard them speaking in tongues and praising God. Then Peter asked, "Can anyone object to their being baptized, now that they have received the Holy Spirit*

just as we did?" So he gave orders for them to be baptized in the name of Jesus Christ.
God is in the change business. Leaders are, by definition, also in the change business. Whether you are helping others change raw materials into finished product, changing people from uneducated to educated, or leading through political and social change, you need to understand both the necessity and tensions of change that come with your calling as a leader.

Acts 15:1-2 *While Paul and Barnabas were at Antioch of Syria, some men from Judea arrived and began to teach the Christians: "Unless you keep the ancient Jewish custom of circumcision taught by Moses, you cannot be saved." Paul and Barnabas, disagreeing with them, argued forcefully and at length. Finally, Paul and Barnabas were sent to Jerusalem, accompanied by some local believers, to talk to the apostles and elders about this question.*
One of the primary tasks of a leader is responding to, initiating, and managing change. Jesus' early followers faced major changes, especially as the Gentiles entered into the community of faith. As they dealt with change, they discovered greater riches in their effectiveness and in their fellowship.

PROMISES FROM GOD Isaiah 40:8 *The grass withers, and the flowers fade, but the word of our God stands forever.*

2 Corinthians 5:17 *Those who become Christians become new persons. They are not the same anymore, for the old life is gone. A new life has begun!*

CHARACTER

See also **HYPOCRISY, INTEGRITY, REPUTATION**

Why does a leader's character matter?

Ezekiel 18:5-9 *Suppose a certain man is just and does what is lawful and right, and . . . does not commit adultery. . . . Suppose he is a merciful creditor . . . and does not rob the poor but instead gives food to the hungry and provides clothes for people in need. And suppose he grants loans without interest, stays away from injustice, is honest and fair when judging others, and faithfully obeys my laws and regulations. Anyone who does these things is just and will surely live, says the Sovereign Lord.*

People often argue that a leader's personal life does not really matter so long as he or she performs the job well. God, however, does not make a distinction between our public and private lives. Justice, righteousness, integrity, mercy, honesty, fairness, and faithfulness are essential traits of a godly leader's character because they reflect who a person really is. They also demonstrate that the leader understands what is truly important in life—loving, honoring, and respecting God and others.

1 Corinthians 4:5 *So be careful not to jump to conclusions before the Lord returns as to whether or not someone is faithful. When the Lord comes, he will bring our deepest secrets to light and will reveal our private motives. And then God will give to everyone whatever praise is due.*

Sometimes leaders are tempted to believe that they are exempt from the standards to which all others are subjected. They may abuse their privileges as leader. But you must remember that whatever is hidden will be revealed.

1 Thessalonians 2:6-10 *As for praise, we have never asked for it from you or anyone else. As apostles of Christ we certainly had a right to make some demands of you, but we were as gentle among you as a mother feeding and caring for her own children. We loved you so much that we gave you not only God's Good News but our own lives, too. . . . You yourselves are our witnesses—and so is God—that we were pure and honest and faultless toward all of you believers.*
Character gives credibility. As a leader, your life will either verify or nullify your life work.

PROMISE FROM GOD Galatians 5:22-23 *But when the Holy Spirit controls our lives, he will produce this kind of fruit in us: love, joy, peace, patience, kindness, goodness, faithfulness, gentleness, and self-control.*

CHEATING

See also **DECEIT, DECEPTION, INTEGRITY**

Why does cheating, on a large or small scale, matter to God?
Proverbs 11:1 *The Lord hates cheating, but he delights in honesty.*
Cheating violates a holy God. Leaders who want God's blessing must abide by God's standards of fairness and justice.

Mark 12:40 *They shamelessly cheat widows out of their property, and then, to cover up the kind of people they really are, they make long prayers in public. Because of this, their punishment will be the greater.*
Leaders who claim faith but are not faithful are hypocrites who will be condemned. They sin first by

cheating and then by trying to cover it with pious acts. God hates both.

Luke 16:10 *Unless you are faithful in small matters, you won't be faithful in large ones. If you cheat even a little, you won't be honest with greater responsibilities.*
Character is tested in the small choices leaders make. Little cheating is cut out of the same piece of cloth as big cheating.

PROMISE FROM GOD Romans 13:9-10 *The commandments against adultery and murder and stealing and coveting—and any other commandment—are all summed up in this one commandment: "Love your neighbor as yourself." Love does no wrong to anyone, so love satisfies all of God's requirements.*

CHOICES

See **DECISIONS**

CHURCH DISCIPLINE

What is the purpose of church discipline?
Proverbs 3:11-12 *My child, don't ignore it when the Lord disciplines you, and don't be discouraged when he corrects you. For the Lord corrects those he loves, just as a father corrects a child in whom he delights.*

Deuteronomy 8:5 *So you should realize that just as a parent disciplines a child, the Lord your God disciplines you to help you.*
Leaders take responsibility for the right actions of the group they lead. When this involves the church, it is

especially important for the integrity of the body of believers and for their witness to the world. Such discipline is based on accountability and consequences. Church discipline is similar to God's discipline or parental discipline. It should be done from a desire to restore rather than to condemn.

How should believers exercise church discipline?

Matthew 18:15 *If another believer sins against you, go privately and point out the fault. If the other person listens and confesses it, you have won that person back.*

James 5:20 *You can be sure that the one who brings that person back will save that sinner from death and bring about the forgiveness of many sins.*
Leaders keep in mind that church discipline is for the benefit of the one being disciplined. Therefore it begins with the personal confrontation between the individuals involved. It moves to the next level only if the person refuses to respond with repentance and restitution.

Hebrews 12:15 *Look after each other so that none of you will miss out on the special favor of God. Watch out that no bitter root of unbelief rises up among you, for whenever it springs up, many are corrupted by its poison.*

1 Corinthians 5:6 *How terrible that you should boast about your spirituality, and yet you let this sort of thing go on. Don't you realize that if even one person is allowed to go on sinning, soon all will be affected?*
Church discipline is also for the benefit of the church body. Restoring one member heals the whole body of believers, just as healing one part of a person's body restores wholeness to the entire body.

Why is church discipline necessary?

Titus 1:13 *Rebuke them as sternly as necessary to make them strong in the faith.*
Church discipline is necessary to maintain strong faith and sound doctrine.

2 Thessalonians 3:11-15 *Yet we hear that some of you are living idle lives, refusing to work and wasting time meddling in other people's business. In the name of the Lord Jesus Christ, we appeal to such people—no, we command them: Settle down and get to work. Earn your own living. And I say to the rest of you, dear brothers and sisters, never get tired of doing good. Take note of those who refuse to obey what we say in this letter. . . . Speak to them as you would to a Christian who needs to be warned.*
Church discipline is necessary to correct disorder that comes from undisciplined lifestyles. One dysfunctional member can disrupt the whole body.

1 Timothy 5:20 *Anyone who sins should be rebuked in front of the whole church so that others will have a proper fear of God.*
Church discipline is necessary as a warning to others to live obediently and to restore relationships with God and others. Discipline always warns about unpleasant consequences.

1 Corinthians 5:3-5, 13 *Concerning the one who has done this, I have already passed judgment in the name of the Lord Jesus. You are to call a meeting of the church, and I will be there in spirit, and the power of the Lord Jesus will be with you as you meet. Then you must cast this man out of the church and into Satan's hands, so that his sinful nature will be destroyed and he himself will be saved when the Lord returns. . . . God will judge those on*

the outside; but as the Scriptures say, "You must remove the evil person from among you."

Church discipline is sometimes necessary to remove the cancer of wickedness. If a member is living in sin and refusing to repent, that person must be removed from the congregation before the evil infects the whole body. Otherwise, the church would be endorsing that sinful act. This is painful surgery, but most surgery is painful. It is important to note that this passage is speaking about those who *willfully* sin against the words of Scripture. These people refuse, over a period of time, to obey God's Word. This is not talking about an individual act of sin where repentance is expected and comes quickly.

When is church discipline appropriate?

1 Timothy 1:20 *Hymenaeus and Alexander are two examples of this. I turned them over to Satan so they would learn not to blaspheme God.*

2 John 10-11 *If someone comes to your meeting and does not teach the truth about Christ, don't invite him into your house or encourage him in any way. Anyone who encourages him becomes a partner in his evil work.*

2 Thessalonians 3:14-15 *Take note of those who refuse to obey what we say in this letter. Stay away from them so they will be ashamed. Don't think of them as enemies, but speak to them as you would to a Christian who needs to be warned.*

Romans 16:17 *And now I make one more appeal, my dear brothers and sisters. Watch out for people who cause divisions and upset people's faith by teaching things that are contrary to what you have been taught. Stay away from them.*

2 Corinthians 13:1-2 *This is the third time I am coming to visit you. As the Scriptures say, "The facts of every case must be established by the testimony of two or three witnesses." I have already warned those who had been sinning when I was there on my second visit. Now I again warn them and all others, just as I did before, that this next time I will not spare them.*

The sins listed in these examples are outwardly evident, dishonoring to Christ publicly, and being continually practiced over time. Those involved have refused to respond in repentance after being verbally confronted. Church discipline is essential in such cases.

PROMISE FROM GOD Jude 22-24 *Show mercy to those whose faith is wavering. Rescue others by snatching them from the flames of judgment. There are still others to whom you need to show mercy, but be careful that you aren't contaminated by their sins. And now, all glory to God, who is able to keep you from stumbling, and who will bring you into his glorious presence innocent of sin and with great joy.*

CHURCH LEADERS

See **DEACONS, ELDERS, PASTORS/MINISTERS**

CODEPENDENCY

See also **CONTROL**

How do leaders avoid codependence?

Matthew 19:16-22 *Someone came to Jesus with this question: "Teacher, what good things must I do to have eternal life?" . . . Jesus told him, "If you want to be perfect, go and sell all you have and give the money to the poor, and you will have treasure in heaven. Then come, follow me." But when the young man heard this, he went sadly away because he had many possessions.*

Codependence means that a person acts in an unhealthy way by protecting people from the consequences of their own actions. Leaders are often tempted to codependence. You may be tempted to compromise your standards, be captive to the crowd's opinion, or give in to the loudest voices, the most insistent demands, or the most fearful pleas. But you must stand your ground. Jesus let this young man walk away. Jesus did not try to talk him into commitment, nor did he lower his requirements.

John 13:21-30 *Now Jesus was in great anguish of spirit, and he exclaimed, "The truth is, one of you will betray me!" . . . Then Jesus told him, "Hurry. Do it now." . . . So Judas left at once, going out into the night.*

Leaders cannot protect people from the consequences of their choices. Jesus let Judas go through with the betrayal, just as he let Peter go through with his denial. The Lord respects a person's will and decision. This is perhaps the hardest part of leadership—letting others fail. But it is also a necessary part.

PROMISE FROM GOD Romans 6:23 *For the wages of sin is death, but the free gift of God is eternal life through Christ Jesus our Lord.*

COMMITMENT

See also **LOYALTY**

What should be my main commitments as a Christian leader?

Matthew 22:37-38 *"You must love the Lord your God with all your heart, all your soul, and all your mind." This is the first and greatest commandment.*

John 6:66-69 *At this point many of his disciples turned away and deserted him. Then Jesus turned to the Twelve and asked, "Are you going to leave, too?" Simon Peter replied, "Lord, to whom would we go? You alone have the words that give eternal life. We believe them, and we know you are the Holy One of God."*

Your first commitment as a Christian leader is to love and honor God in all you do.

Matthew 22:39 *A second is equally important: "Love your neighbor as yourself."*

John 13:34-35 *So now I am giving you a new commandment: Love each other. Just as I have loved you, you should love each other. Your love for one another will prove to the world that you are my disciples.*

Your second commitment as a Christian leader is to love God's people.

John 15:5 *Yes, I am the vine; you are the branches. Those who remain in me, and I in them, will produce much fruit. For apart from me you can do nothing.*

Your third commitment as a Christian leader is to serve the Lord by continuing Christ's work in the world.

What should my commitments look like?

Luke 9:57-58 *As they were walking along someone*

said to Jesus, "I will follow you no matter where you go." But Jesus replied, "Foxes have dens to live in, and birds have nests, but I, the Son of Man, have no home of my own, not even a place to lay my head."

Luke 14:27 *And you cannot be my disciple if you do not carry your own cross and follow me.*
You must be the most committed of the group. Jesus' high standards model the kind of commitment he expects in all areas of life, especially in your undivided loyalty to him. Leaders cannot expect special treatment. You are not exempt from the same standards that apply to those you lead.

Romans 6:13 *Give yourselves completely to God since you have been given new life. And use your whole body as a tool to do what is right for the glory of God.*
Your wholehearted commitment involves giving God everything, even your body, to use as he wishes.

PROMISE FROM GOD Hebrews 3:14 *For if we are faithful to the end, . . . we will share in all that belongs to Christ.*

COMMUNICATION

See also **WORDS**

How can I best communicate with others?
2 Corinthians 6:11-13 *Oh, dear Corinthian friends! We have spoken honestly with you. Our hearts are open to you. If there is a problem between us, it is not because of a lack of love on our part, but because you have withheld your love from us. I am talking now as I would to my own children. Open your hearts to us!*

Do not keep secrets, but rather confront issues tactfully, but directly. Leaders are committed to open, candid communication with those they lead and serve.

Galatians 6:1 *Dear brothers and sisters, if another Christian is overcome by some sin, you who are godly should gently and humbly help that person back onto the right path.*

1 Thessalonians 2:7 *As apostles of Christ we certainly had a right to make some demands of you, but we were as gentle among you as a mother feeding and caring for her own children.*

When you know there is a problem, get involved, being kind and gentle in the process. Leaders pay attention and listen to the needs and struggles of those around them.

Isaiah 50:4 *The Sovereign Lord has given me his words of wisdom, so that I know what to say to all these weary ones. Morning by morning he wakens me and opens my understanding to his will.*

Be a person of the Word and of prayer. Leaders seek the Lord's wisdom and understanding in addressing the various needs and issues they face.

Acts 23:1 *Gazing intently at the high council, Paul began: "Brothers, I have always lived before God in all good conscience!"*

Keep your own conscience clear. Leaders have the credibility of a clear conscience so that they are able to convey their interest and attention with their body language—especially being able to look others in the eye.

Colossians 4:6 *Let your conversation be gracious and effective so that you will have the right answer for everyone.*

Ephesians 4:29 *Don't use foul or abusive language. Let everything you say be good and helpful, so that your words will be an encouragement to those who hear them.*
Watch your language. Leaders' words are to be gracious, effective, good, helpful, and encouraging to others.

Proverbs 13:17 *An unreliable messenger stumbles into trouble, but a reliable messenger brings healing.*
Be trustworthy and reliable. Leaders must be a reliable source of communication.

2 Corinthians 1:13 *My letters have been straightforward, and there is nothing written between the lines and nothing you can't understand.*
Be clear. Leaders are to be straightforward and clear so they can increase understanding and help people grow to spiritual maturity.

2 Corinthians 6:4 *In everything we do we try to show that we are true ministers of God.*
Remember that what you do may speak much more eloquently than what you say. Leaders communicate their commitment to Christ through their lifestyle.

What are the side effects of poor communication?
James 3:5-6 *The tongue is a small thing, but what enormous damage it can do. A tiny spark can set a great forest on fire. And the tongue is a flame of fire. It is full of wickedness that can ruin your whole life. It can turn the entire course of your life into a blazing flame of destruction, for it is set on fire by hell itself.*

2 Timothy 2:23 *Don't get involved in foolish, ignorant arguments that only start fights.*

Proverbs 26:6 *Trusting a fool to convey a message is as foolish as cutting off one's feet or drinking poison!* Poor communication can lead to a lack of control, quarrels, evil actions, and foolishness.

PROMISES FROM GOD Proverbs 10:20 *The words of the godly are like sterling silver.*

Ephesians 4:29 *Let everything you say be good and helpful, so that your words will be an encouragement to those who hear them.*

COMMUNITY

Why should a leader be committed to developing community?

1 Samuel 22:1-2 *So David left Gath and escaped to the cave of Adullam. Soon his brothers and other relatives joined him there. Then others began coming—men who were in trouble or in debt or who were just discontented—until David was the leader of about four hundred men.*

Mark 3:13-14 *Afterward Jesus went up on a mountain and called the ones he wanted to go with him. And they came to him. Then he selected twelve of them to be his regular companions, calling them apostles.*

Mark 6:6-7 *Then Jesus went out from village to village, teaching. And he called his twelve disciples together and sent them out two by two.*

Acts 11:25-26 *Then Barnabas went on to Tarsus to find Saul. When he found him, he brought him back to Antioch. Both of them stayed there with the church for a full year, teaching great numbers of people.* Leaders are often tempted to be lone rangers. But whether or not you are in a specifically Christian setting, community is essential for effective leadership. In fact, leadership can be defined in part as "accomplishment through community." Leaders get things done through others. The Bible has countless examples of leaders who developed community in large and small groups in order to fulfill God's will.

Acts 15:24-26 *We understand that some men from here have troubled you and upset you with their teaching, but they had no such instructions from us. So it seemed good to us, having unanimously agreed on our decision, to send you these official representatives, along with our beloved Barnabas and Paul, who have risked their lives for the sake of our Lord Jesus Christ.*
The early church modeled a process that respected all people involved and cultivated healthy community in the midst of conflict. Leaders do not lead in a vacuum, and the "product" they are trying to produce is not all that matters. The people are the ultimate product; therefore processes that involve and respect the community are important.

What is the value of community?
Acts 9:26-28 *When Saul arrived in Jerusalem, he tried to meet with the believers, but they were all afraid of him. They thought he was only pretending to be a believer! Then Barnabas brought him to the apostles and told them how Saul had seen the Lord on the way to Damascus. Barnabas also told them what the Lord had said to Saul and how he boldly preached in the name of Jesus in Damascus. Then the apostles accepted Saul, and after that he was constantly with them in Jerusalem, preaching boldly in the name of the Lord.*
Community can provide trustworthy references as to other people's integrity and character.

Acts 13:1-3 *Among the prophets and teachers of the church at Antioch of Syria were Barnabas, Simeon (called "the black man"), Lucius (from Cyrene), Manaen (the childhood companion of King Herod Antipas), and Saul. One day as these men were worshiping the Lord and fasting, the Holy Spirit said, "Dedicate Barnabas and Saul for the special work I have for them." So after more fasting and prayer, the men laid their hands on them and sent them on their way.*
Community can help leaders to discern gifts and call. It is also interesting to note that the early church community was marked by leaders who were a mix of races and socio-economic status. This is a model of community the world needs to see at every level.

Galatians 6:2 *Share each other's troubles and problems, and in this way obey the law of Christ.*
Community means that people share each other's difficulties in life and mutually support one another.

Acts 2:44 *And all the believers met together constantly and shared everything they had.*
Community provides a practical way to meet one another's needs.

James 5:16 *Confess your sins to each other and pray for each other so that you may be healed.*
Community provides accountability and spiritual support.

1 Thessalonians 5:11-13 *So encourage each other and build each other up, just as you are already doing. Dear brothers and sisters, honor those who are your leaders in the Lord's work. They work hard among you and warn you against all that is wrong. Think highly of them and give them your wholehearted love because of their work.*

Community provides encouragement and practical support.

PROMISE FROM GOD Matthew 18:20 *For where two or three gather together because they are mine, I am there among them.*

COMPARISONS

See also **COMPETITION**

How can comparing myself to others affect me as a leader?

John 21:21-22 *Peter asked Jesus, "What about him, Lord?" Jesus replied, "If I want him to remain alive until I return, what is that to you? You follow me."*
Comparing yourself to others takes your focus off of Jesus.

1 Samuel 8:20 *We want to be like the nations around us. Our king will govern us and lead us into battle.*
Comparing yourself to others and wanting what they have may cause you to miss what God wants for you.

Luke 18:11 *The proud Pharisee stood by himself and prayed this prayer: "I thank you, God, that I am not a sinner like everyone else, especially like that tax collector over there!"*
Comparing yourself to others may lead to false righteousness, leading you to think you are better than someone else.

Why is comparison foolish?

1 Corinthians 12:18-27 *God made our bodies with many parts, and he has put each part just where he wants it. . . . Some of the parts that seem weakest and least*

important are really the most necessary. And the parts we regard as less honorable are those we clothe with the greatest care. . . . If one part suffers, all the parts suffer with it, and if one part is honored, all the parts are glad. Now all of you together are Christ's body, and each one of you is a separate and necessary part of it.

Even as the parts of the body cannot be compared, so you are foolish to compare yourself with others. Each person is created by God to serve a role in his kingdom. As a leader, it is especially important that you not be driven by the anxiety or pride of comparison. Likewise, you should not distract those you lead by comparisons.

How can I refuse the temptation to compare?

1 Corinthians 3:5, 9 *Each of us did the work the Lord gave us. . . . We work together as partners who belong to God.*

You can be freed from the need to compare by accepting and celebrating your particular calling from God. Realize that no one can do it all and that God has given you the privilege of being part of his work, while others have their own parts to play.

Romans 14:10, 12 *So why do you condemn another Christian? Why do you look down on another Christian? Remember, each of us will stand personally before the judgment seat of God. . . . Yes, each of us will have to give a personal account to God.*

God looks at us individually. Your neighbor will give his own account to God. You will give your own account to God. We will not give account for one another.

Galatians 6:4-5 *Be sure to do what you should, for then you will enjoy the personal satisfaction of having done*

your work well, and you won't need to compare yourself to anyone else. For we are each responsible for our own conduct.
Examine your own faith and actions. What others do or don't do ultimately has no bearing on your relationship with or on your responsibility to God.

Romans 12:15 *When others are happy, be happy with them. If they are sad, share their sorrow.*
Rejoice with others in their successes; don't wish their successes were yours.

PROMISE FROM GOD Psalm 89:6 *For who in all of heaven can compare with the Lord? What mightiest angel is anything like the Lord?*

COMPASSION

Why is compassion an important quality of leadership?
Mark 1:40-41 *A man with leprosy came and knelt in front of Jesus, begging to be healed. "If you want to, you can make me well again," he said. Moved with pity, Jesus touched him. "I want to," he said. "Be healed!"*

Luke 6:36 *You must be compassionate, just as your Father is compassionate.*
A mark of godly leaders is to show the kind of compassion that God shows to you.

2 Samuel 9:7 *But David said, "Don't be afraid! I've asked you to come so that I can be kind to you because of my vow to your father, Jonathan."*
Leaders honor God and others by their acts of compassion. David's compassion to Jonathan's son (Saul's

grandson), Mephibosheth, showed his gracious heart, generosity, and integrity. It honored Jonathan, helped Mephibosheth, and secured the loyalty of Saul's descendents.

What happens if I fail to show compassion?

Ezekiel 34:2 *Give them this message from the Sovereign Lord: Destruction is certain for you shepherds who feed yourselves instead of your flocks.*

Leaders who are too busy to care for people will soon cease to be effective leaders. The failure of compassion leads to danger for the people in your care as well as to God's judgment on your selfishness.

PROMISE FROM GOD Psalm 145:9 *The Lord is good to everyone. He showers compassion on all his creation.*

COMPETITION

See also **COMPARISONS, ENVY, JEALOUSY**

What are the dangers of competition?

Numbers 12:1-2 *While they were at Hazeroth, Miriam and Aaron criticized Moses because he had married a Cushite woman. They said, "Has the Lord spoken only through Moses? Hasn't he spoken through us, too?" But the Lord heard them.*

Competition disrupts not only your relationship with others, but also your relationship with God. Miriam and Aaron, who were also leaders during the exodus, were jealous of their brother Moses and were competing for the attention and recognition Moses received. But their competition would bring them under God's judgment.

Mark 9:38-40 *John said to Jesus, "Teacher, we saw a man using your name to cast out demons, but we told him to stop because he isn't one of our group." "Don't stop him!" Jesus said. "No one who performs miracles in my name will soon be able to speak evil of me. Anyone who is not against us is for us."*
Leaders must beware of the competition their followers feel on their behalf. The disciples did not want to permit others to minister who weren't doing it exactly their way. But Jesus called them to celebrate instead of compete.

Matthew 18:1-4 *About that time the disciples came to Jesus and asked, "Which of us is greatest in the Kingdom of Heaven?" . . . Then [Jesus] said, ". . . Anyone who becomes as humble as this little child is the greatest in the Kingdom of Heaven."*
Leadership is about service, not personal advancement. Competition is fueled by pride, whereas the commitment to serve is fueled by humility.

How should I respond when others compete with me?
Numbers 12:4-6 *Immediately the Lord called to Moses, Aaron, and Miriam and said, "Go out to the Tabernacle, all three of you!" And the three of them went out. Then the Lord descended in the pillar of cloud and stood at the entrance of the Tabernacle. "Aaron and Miriam!" he called, and they stepped forward. And the Lord said to them, "Now listen to me!"*
You will be tempted to defend yourself when others compete with or attack you. Moses allowed God to vindicate his leadership. Rather than continually defending yourself, trust God to validate your leadership.

How should I respond when I am tempted to compete?

Philippians 1:15-18 *Some are preaching out of jealousy and rivalry. But others preach about Christ with pure motives. They preach because they love me, for they know the Lord brought me here to defend the Good News. Those others do not have pure motives as they preach about Christ. They preach with selfish ambition, not sincerely, intending to make my chains more painful to me. But whether or not their motives are pure, the fact remains that the message about Christ is being preached, so I rejoice. And I will continue to rejoice.*

Keep your focus on the goal, not on your own popularity or standing in the polls. Remember that the Lord is number one, not you. Paul refused to condemn those who were competing with him. Keep the goal in mind and trust God to deal with others. God will work through them—or in spite of them!

PROMISE FROM GOD Romans 12:5 *We are all parts of his one body, and each of us has different work to do. And since we are all one body in Christ, we belong to each other, and each of us needs all the others.*

CONFIDENCE

Where do leaders get their confidence?

Psalm 118:8 *It is better to trust the Lord than to put confidence in people.*

Confidence comes from knowing that God is completely trustworthy.

Zechariah 4:6 *Then he said to me, "This is what the Lord says to Zerubbabel: It is not by force nor by strength, but by my Spirit, says the Lord Almighty."*
Confidence comes from God's presence, power, and provision, not your own cleverness, talent, or resources.

Philippians 4:13 *For I can do everything with the help of Christ who gives me the strength I need.*
Confidence is not pride, but security in Christ. That security is based on God's call on your life, and in the exercise of the gifts he has given you.

How does a leader's confidence affect others?
1 Kings 18:36-39 *Elijah the prophet walked up to the altar and prayed, "O Lord, . . . prove today that you are God in Israel and that I am your servant. Prove that I have done all this at your command." . . . Immediately the fire of the Lord flashed down from heaven and burned up the young bull, the wood, the stones, and the dust. It even licked up all the water in the ditch! And when the people saw it, they fell on their faces and cried out, "The Lord is God! The Lord is God!"*
A leader's confidence in God can literally change everything. Elijah's boldness on Mount Carmel began to liberate the nation from the wicked influence of Baal worship.

PROMISE FROM GOD John 16:33 *Here on earth you will have many trials and sorrows. But take heart, because I have overcome the world.*

CONFLICT

See also **ANGER, BETRAYAL, CONFRONTATION, FORGIVENESS**

What causes conflict?

Proverbs 13:10 *Pride leads to arguments.*

Proverbs 28:25 *Greed causes fighting.*

Proverbs 30:33 *Anger causes quarrels.*

James 4:1 *What is causing the quarrels and fights among you? Isn't it the whole army of evil desires at war within you?*
While there are countless reasons for conflict, some of the most common include pride, greed, and anger. These aspects of our sinful, human nature bring us into conflict with other people.

Matthew 23:23 *How terrible it will be for you teachers of religious law and you Pharisees. Hypocrites!*
There are times when leaders cannot ignore situations and actually need to initiate conflict in order to speak for truth and justice. Jesus confronted the Pharisees not only for their hypocritical behavior, but also because of their destructive influence as teachers and leaders.

How can I best handle conflict?

Genesis 13:8-9 *"This arguing between our herdsmen has got to stop," [Abram] said. . . . "I'll tell you what we'll do."*
You can take the initiative to manage and hopefully resolve conflict. Abram gave Lot first choice, putting family peace above personal desires.

Genesis 26:21-22 *Isaac's men then dug another well, but again there was a fight over it. . . . He dug another well, and the local people finally left him alone.* Solving conflict takes humility, a desire to see peace more than personal victory.

Acts 15:37-38 *Barnabas agreed and wanted to take along John Mark. But Paul disagreed strongly, since John Mark had deserted them in Pamphylia and had not shared in their work. Their disagreement over this was so sharp that they separated. Barnabas took John Mark with him and sailed for Cyprus.*
In conflict, it's important to keep the focus on the problem, not on the people. In this circumstance, it appears that Barnabas understood this, while Paul was still struggling with John Mark's desertion.

PROMISE FROM GOD Psalm 55:18 *He rescues me and keeps me safe from the battle waged against me, even though many still oppose me.*

CONFRONTATION

See also **CONFLICT, CRITICISM**

Under what circumstances should leaders confront others?
Ephesians 5:11 *Take no part in the worthless deeds of evil and darkness; instead, rebuke and expose them.* Leaders confront evil and wickedness so that these problems don't infect the entire group.

Luke 17:3 *If another believer sins, rebuke him; then if he repents, forgive him.*

Confronting someone who does wrong may lead that person back into reconciliation with God and others.

How can I effectively confront others?

Matthew 18:15-17 *If another believer sins against you, go privately and point out the fault. . . . If your are unsuccessful, take one or two others with you and go back again. . . . If that person still refuses to listen, take your case to the church.*

Nehemiah 13:11 *I immediately confronted the leaders and demanded, "Why has the Temple of God been neglected?"*

When you realize that you have a significant problem, you should confront those involved as soon as possible.

Titus 3:2 *They must not speak evil of anyone, and they must avoid quarreling. Instead, they should be gentle and show true humility to everyone.*

The manner of confrontation is as important as the content. It is essential to consider how you would want someone to speak to you about a problem in your life.

Proverbs 27:5 *An open rebuke is better than hidden love!*

2 Timothy 2:24-25 *The Lord's servants must not quarrel but must be kind to everyone. They must be able to teach effectively and be patient with difficult people. They should gently teach those who oppose the truth. Perhaps God will change those people's hearts, and they will believe the truth.*

Confront openly, but without quarreling. Be kind and trust God to change the person's heart!

2 Timothy 1:7 *God has not given us a spirit of fear and timidity, but of power, love, and self-discipline.*

If confrontation is necessary, trust God to give you the power, love, and self-discipline to say what you must.

How should I respond when others confront me?
Proverbs 19:25 *If you punish a mocker, the simple-minded will learn a lesson; if you reprove the wise, they will be all the wiser.*
Confrontation should increase your wisdom.

Proverbs 24:26 *It is an honor to receive an honest reply.*
You should be honored that someone cares enough about you to want what is best for you.

PROMISE FROM GOD Proverbs 17:10 *A single rebuke does more for a person of understanding than a hundred lashes on the back of a fool.*

CONTENTMENT

How can leaders find contentment regardless of life's circumstances?
2 Corinthians 12:10 *Since I know it is all for Christ's good, I am quite content with my weaknesses and with insults, hardships, persecutions, and calamities.*

Philippians 4:11-13 *I have learned how to get along happily whether I have much or little. I know how to live on almost nothing or with everything. I have learned the secret of living in every situation, whether it is with a full stomach or empty, with plenty or little. For I can do everything with the help of Christ who gives me the strength I need.*
Leaders are often people who find it difficult to be content. A mixture of vision, ambition (holy and

sometimes not so holy!), and drive can make you restless. But God's Word teaches that when you depend on circumstances for your contentment, you become unhappy when things don't go your way. When you depend on Jesus for your contentment, you are secure because he never fails.

Psalm 107:8-9 *Let them praise the Lord for his great love and for all his wonderful deeds to them. For he satisfies the thirsty and fills the hungry with good things.*

Psalm 119:35 *Make me walk along the path of your commands, for that is where my happiness is found.*

Psalm 90:14 *Satisfy us in the morning with your unfailing love, so we may sing for joy to the end of our lives.*
God, who is the source of every good thing, can certainly satisfy your needs and give you contentment.

Isaiah 26:3 *You will keep in perfect peace all who trust in you, whose thoughts are fixed on you!*
There are many ways to have peace, or what you think is peace, but genuine peace is found only in a trusting relationship with the Lord.

1 Timothy 6:6-7 *Yet true religion with contentment is great wealth. After all, we didn't bring anything with us when we came into the world, and we certainly cannot carry anything with us when we die.*
Contentment comes from keeping an eternal perspective.

What is the relationship between wealth and contentment?

1 Timothy 6:17 *Tell those who are rich in this world not to be proud and not to trust in their money, which will soon be gone. But their trust should be in the living God, who richly gives us all we need for our enjoyment.*

Ecclesiastes 5:10 *Those who love money will never have enough. How absurd to think that wealth brings true happiness!*
Leaders are often closely involved with financial matters and may experience material blessings. But you must not allow money and possessions to deceive you into thinking, "If only I had a little more, I would be content." Nothing could be further from the truth.

Hebrews 13:5 *Stay away from the love of money; be satisfied with what you have. For God has said, "I will never fail you. I will never forsake you."*
Contentment is not related to how much material wealth you have but to how much of God's presence is in your life.

Proverbs 30:7-9 *O God, I beg two favors from you before I die. First, help me never to tell a lie. Second, give me neither poverty nor riches! Give me just enough to satisfy my needs. For if I grow rich, I may deny you and say, "Who is the Lord?" And if I am too poor, I may steal and thus insult God's holy name.*
You can ask God for the contentment that keeps you in the way of holiness and obedience.

PROMISE FROM GOD 2 Peter 1:3 *As we know Jesus better, his divine power gives us everything we need for living a godly life. He has called us to receive his own glory and goodness!*

CONTROL

See also **CODEPENDENCY**

How does the Bible advise leaders to deal with controlling people?

Genesis 30:25-27 *Soon after Joseph was born to Rachel, Jacob said to Laban, "I want to go back home." . . . "Please don't leave me," Laban replied.*
Jacob finally broke free from Laban's control by a combination of confrontation, patience, and shrewd negotiation.

3 John 10 *He not only refuses to welcome the traveling teachers, he also tells others not to help them.*
As John advises in this passage, leaders are to confront those who control others for selfish reasons. You must never sacrifice the truth or the good of the whole church for one selfish and controlling person. However, any such confrontation must be handled with love (see Ephesians 4:15).

Galatians 4:17 *Those false teachers who are so anxious to win your favor are not doing it for your good.*
Paul confronted those who sought inappropriate and destructive control of the early church.

How can I exercise appropriate control without being controlling?

Deuteronomy 30:19 *Today I have given you the choice between life and death, between blessings and curses. I call on heaven and earth to witness the choice you make. Oh, that you would choose life, that you and your descendants might live!*
Leaders are responsible to people without taking responsibility away from them. This is what is meant

by being in control without being controlling. Moses did all he could to persuade the people to choose the way of life, but in the end he knew that the choice was theirs to make.

Jude 24 *And now, all glory to God, who is able to keep you from stumbling, and who will bring you into his glorious presence innocent of sin and with great joy.*
Leaders find their greatest confidence in God's preserving power. This enables you to let go and trust God with people and circumstances.

PROMISES FROM GOD Psalm 86:9 *All the nations—and you made each one—will come and bow before you, Lord; they will praise your great and holy name.*

Galatians 5:22-23 *But when the Holy Spirit controls our lives, he will produce this kind of fruit in us: love, joy, peace, . . . and self-control.*

COUNSEL/COUNSELORS

See also **ADVICE/ADVISERS, DECISIONS, WISDOM**

Why is it important for leaders to seek godly counsel?
Proverbs 12:15 *Fools think they need no advice, but the wise listen to others.*

Proverbs 13:10 *Pride leads to arguments; those who take advice are wise.*

Proverbs 11:14 *Without wise leadership, a nation falls; with many counselors, there is safety.*

Proverbs 15:22 *Plans go wrong for lack of advice; many counselors bring success.*

Proverbs 20:18 *Plans succeed through good counsel; don't go to war without the advice of others.*
Leaders continually face complex problems that involve a number of variables and options. The wise seek the counsel and expertise of others. Fools are too proud or ignorant to understand the needs and risks.

How can I know that God will give me counsel?
Matthew 7:7, 11 *Keep on asking, and you will be given what you ask for. Keep on looking, and you will find. Keep on knocking, and the door will be opened. . . . If you sinful people know how to give good gifts to your children, how much more will your heavenly Father give good gifts to those who ask him.*

James 1:5 *If you need wisdom—if you want to know what God wants you to do—ask him, and he will gladly tell you.*
God's Word consistently invites you to ask for the wisdom and direction you need. With all the people and circumstances that depend on you, it is imperative that you as a leader continually seek God's counsel.

What are the characteristics of God's counsel?
Job 12:13 *But true wisdom and power are with God; counsel and understanding are his.*

Proverbs 8:14 *Good advice and success belong to me. Insight and strength are mine.*
God's counsel is true wisdom, understanding, and insight.

Psalm 32:8 *The Lord says, "I will guide you along the best pathway for your life. I will advise you and watch over you."*
God's counsel leads to the best way to live.

Psalm 73:24 *You will keep on guiding me with your counsel, leading me to a glorious destiny.*
God's counsel is ongoing and eternal.

Psalm 33:11 *But the Lord's plans stand firm forever; his intentions can never be shaken.*

Isaiah 46:10 *Only I can tell you what is going to happen even before it happens. Everything I plan will come to pass, for I do whatever I wish.*

Isaiah 14:24, 27 *The Lord Almighty has sworn this oath: "It will all happen as I have planned. It will come about according to my purposes. . . . The Lord Almighty has spoken—who can change his plans? When his hand moves, who can stop him?"*
God's counsel is sure. You can always count on it to be good and wise and right.

PROMISE FROM GOD Psalm 1:1 *Oh, the joys of those who do not follow the advice of the wicked, or stand around with sinners, or join in with scoffers.*

COURAGE

Where do leaders get the courage to face the challenges and obstacles of life?
Isaiah 41:10 *Don't be afraid, for I am with you. Do not be dismayed, for I am your God. I will strengthen you. I will help you. I will uphold you with my victorious right hand.*

Joshua 1:9 *Be strong and courageous! Do not be afraid or discouraged. For the Lord your God is with you wherever you go.*
Leaders are often in scary situations. You may have a

great deal of money at stake in a decision, or be facing extreme public pressure, or even have the lives of others on the line. True courage comes from turning to God, understanding that he is stronger than your mightiest foes and that he wants to use his strength to help you.

Job 11:18 *You will have courage because you will have hope.*

Numbers 14:6-9 *Two of the men who had explored the land, Joshua son of Nun and Caleb son of Jephunneh, tore their clothing. They said to the community of Israel, "The land we explored is a wonderful land! . . . Don't be afraid of the people of the land. They are only helpless prey to us! They have no protection, but the Lord is with us! Don't be afraid of them!"*
Fear is a part of leadership. Leaders don't escape the emotion of fear, but they learn how to manage the fear so that it doesn't control them. Caleb and Joshua had courage fueled by the promise of God that he was greater than any enemy they faced.

How do I find courage to face those who criticize, intimidate, or threaten me?
Psalm 27:1 *The Lord is my light and my salvation— so why should I be afraid?*

Luke 12:4 *Dear friends, don't be afraid of those who want to kill you. They can only kill the body; they cannot do any more to you.*

1 John 4:4 *But you belong to God, my dear children. You have already won your fight with these false prophets, because the Spirit who lives in you is greater than the spirit who lives in the world.*

1 Samuel 17:32-37 *"Don't worry about a thing," David told Saul. "I'll go fight this Philistine!" "Don't be ridiculous!" Saul replied. "There is no way you can go against this Philistine." . . . But David persisted. "I have been taking care of my father's sheep," he said. "When a lion or a bear comes to steal a lamb from the flock, I go after it with a club and take the lamb from its mouth. If the animal turns on me, I catch it by the jaw and club it to death. I have done this to both lions and bears, and I'll do it to this pagan Philistine, too, for he has defied the armies of the living God! The Lord who saved me from the claws of the lion and the bear will save me from this Philistine!"*
You can find courage from your past experiences of God's faithfulness.

Judges 6:14-16 *Then the Lord turned to him and said, "Go with the strength you have and rescue Israel from the Midianites. I am sending you!" "But Lord," Gideon replied, "how can I rescue Israel? My clan is the weakest in the whole tribe of Manasseh, and I am the least in my entire family!" The Lord said to him, "I will be with you. And you will destroy the Midianites as if you were fighting against one man."*
You can learn that courage comes neither from your qualifications nor your credentials, but from the promise of God's presence and power.

PROMISE FROM GOD Joshua 10:25 *"Don't ever be afraid or discouraged," Joshua told his men. "Be strong and courageous, for the Lord is going to do this to all of your enemies."*

CRISIS

See also **TRIALS/TROUBLE**

How should leaders respond in crisis?

2 Chronicles 20:2-12 *Messengers came and told Jehoshaphat, "A vast army from Edom is marching against you from beyond the Dead Sea." . . . Jehoshaphat stood before the people of Judah and Jerusalem in front of the new courtyard at the Temple of the Lord. He prayed, ". . . O our God, won't you stop them? We are powerless against this mighty army that is about to attack us. We do not know what to do, but we are looking to you for help."*
Leadership is most severely tested in times of crisis. Jehoshaphat faced three attacking armies without the military resources to rebuff them. He turned to prayer as a first response. God delivered the king and his people in a remarkable way. Crises become a powerful means for God to reveal his care and his power on your behalf.

Psalm 46:1 *God is our refuge and strength, always ready to help in times of trouble.*
Leaders must remember that ultimately they can protect neither themselves nor their followers, but God can. Call on the Lord for protection and direction in critical times.

John 16:33 *I have told you all this so that you may have peace in me. Here on earth you will have many trials and sorrows. But take heart, because I have overcome the world.*
Leaders are not surprised by struggles and crises. We live in a fallen world and expect there to be troubles. But along with the troubles comes the strength and wisdom of God to handle them.

How can leaders help to minimize crises?

Proverbs 27:12 *A prudent person foresees the danger ahead and takes precautions. The simpleton goes blindly on and suffers the consequences.*
Sometimes a crisis comes because a leader did not make wise decisions. Taking time to do your best to anticipate the consequences of your actions and decisions will go a long way to minimize the incidence of a crisis.

1 Peter 5:6-10 *So humble yourselves under the mighty power of God, and in his good time he will honor you. Give all your worries and cares to God, for he cares about what happens to you. Be careful! Watch out for attacks from the Devil, your great enemy. He prowls around like a roaring lion, looking for some victim to devour. Take a firm stand against him, and be strong in your faith. . . . After you have suffered a little while, he will restore, support, and strengthen you, and he will place you on a firm foundation.*
The wise leader avoids many crises by leading with humility, complete dependence on God, and awareness of a spiritual enemy. Remember that suffering will not last forever, and that God will restore you.

PROMISE FROM GOD Psalm 119:143 *As pressure and stress bear down on me, I find joy in your commands.*

CRITICISM

See also **ACCUSATIONS, APPROVAL, CONFRONTATION**

How should leaders respond to criticism?

Ecclesiastes 7:5 *It is better to be criticized by a wise person than to be praised by a fool!*

Proverbs 15:31 *If you listen to constructive criticism, you will be at home among the wise.*
Leaders are the most visible and therefore the most vulnerable to criticism. If it comes from a person you deem credible, humble yourself and consider that person's input. Like a coach helping an athlete, candid criticism can help you improve in countless ways.

How should I respond to unjust criticism?

John 19:9-11 *He [Pilate] took Jesus back into the headquarters again and asked him, "Where are you from?" But Jesus gave no answer. "You won't talk to me?" Pilate demanded. "Don't you realize that I have the power to release you or to crucify you?" Then Jesus said, "You would have no power over me at all unless it were given to you from above. So the one who brought me to you has the greater sin."*
You can respond first with silence. Intentional silence can express strength and communicate your desire not to escalate the conflict. A second strategy is to simply state the truth concerning your confidence in your position and even your standing before God.

Galatians 1:10 *Obviously, I'm not trying to be a people pleaser! No, I am trying to please God. If I were still trying to please people, I would not be Christ's servant.*
Human criticism loses much of its power when you focus on pleasing God.

PROMISES FROM GOD Proverbs 12:18 *Some people make cutting remarks, but the words of the wise bring healing.*

1 Peter 4:14 *Be happy if you are insulted for being a Christian, for then the glorious Spirit of God will come upon you.*

DEACONS

See also **ELDERS**

What do deacons do as church leaders?

Acts 6:1-4 *But as the believers rapidly multiplied, there were rumblings of discontent. Those who spoke Greek complained against those who spoke Hebrew, saying that their widows were being discriminated against in the daily distribution of food. So the Twelve called a meeting of all the believers. "We apostles should spend our time preaching and teaching the word of God, not administering a food program," they said. "Now look around among yourselves, brothers, and select seven men who are well respected and are full of the Holy Spirit and wisdom. We will put them in charge of this business. Then we can spend our time in prayer and preaching and teaching the word."*
The position of deacon arose to care for serving and meeting needs in the congregation. Deacons would insure that the congregation cared for people in practical ways.

What is the difference between elders and deacons?

1 Timothy 3:1, 8 *It is a true saying that if someone wants to be an elder, he desires an honorable responsibility. . . . In the same way, deacons must be people who are respected and have integrity.*

Paul does not give precise definitions, but the words themselves give us significant indications of the nature of the roles. The word translated as elder is "overseer," which most likely refers to one who leads through preaching, teaching, and oversight of the congregation. The word for deacon means "one who serves." Acts 6:1-6 describes their role of providing for the practical needs of the early church, but deacons such as Stephen and Philip were also powerful witnesses. As we study the characteristics and qualifications for either role, however, it is obvious that their distinction is a matter of function, not value. Both are seeking to be faithful to God's call as they serve God's people.

PROMISE FROM GOD Proverbs 11:14
Without wise leadership, a nation falls; with many counselors, there is safety.

DEBT

See also **MONEY**

In what ways should leaders be cautious regarding debt?

Proverbs 6:1-3 *My child, if you co-sign a loan for a friend or guarantee the debt of someone you hardly know, . . . you have placed yourself at your friend's mercy.*

Proverbs 22:26-27 *Do not co-sign another person's note or put up a guarantee for someone else's loan. If you can't pay it, even your bed will be snatched from under you.*

Leaders often get involved in financing and loans. God's Word warns us to be cautious in making commitments to co-sign on another's loan. If you co-sign a note, be absolutely sure you can repay the entire debt if your friend defaults on the loan. Otherwise, you will be putting yourself, your business, and even your family at risk.

Proverbs 22:7 *Just as the rich rule the poor, so the borrower is servant to the lender.*
Debt can cause you to be controlled by those to whom you owe.

Psalm 37:21 *The wicked borrow and never repay, but the godly are generous givers.*
To owe and purposefully not pay is wrong; to give even when you are not under obligation pleases God.

Romans 13:7-8 *Give to everyone what you owe them: Pay your taxes and import duties, and give respect and honor to all to whom it is due. Pay all your debts, except the debt of love for others. You can never finish paying that!*
Pay your debts in a timely manner because it is important to honor your commitments. This isn't saying you can never have a home mortgage or car payments, but that when payments are due you must pay them respectfully and honorably.

PROMISE FROM GOD Hebrews 13:5 *Stay away from the love of money; be satisfied with what you have. For God has said, "I will never fail you. I will never forsake you."*

DECEIT/DECEPTION

See also **CHEATING**

How should leaders deal with those who deceive?

Acts 5:1-5, 11 *There was also a man named Ananias who, with his wife, Sapphira, sold some property. He brought part of the money to the apostles, but he claimed it was the full amount. His wife had agreed to this deception. Then Peter said, "Ananias, why has Satan filled your heart? You lied to the Holy Spirit, and you kept some of the money for yourself. The property was yours to sell or not sell, as you wished. And after selling it, the money was yours to give away. How could you do a thing like this? You weren't lying to us but to God." As soon as Ananias heard these words, he fell to the floor and died. . . . Great fear gripped the entire church and all others who heard what had happened.*

Leaders cannot tolerate deception. It corrupts the community. The story of Ananias and Saphira reveals how the leaders, guided by the Holy Spirit, dealt with deception swiftly so that it would not weaken the fledging church. While your situations will not be this extreme, you dare not take deception lightly.

PROMISES FROM GOD Psalm 32:2 *Yes, what joy for those whose record the Lord has cleared of sin, whose lives are lived in complete honesty!*

Proverbs 19:5 *A false witness will not go unpunished, nor will a liar escape.*

DECISIONS

See also **ADVICE/ADVISERS, COUNSEL/COUNSELORS, WISDOM**

How can leaders make good decisions?

Proverbs 1:7 *Fear of the Lord is the beginning of knowledge. Only fools despise wisdom and discipline.*

Proverbs 3:5-6 *Trust in the Lord with all your heart; do not depend on your own understanding. Seek his will in all you do, and he will direct your paths.*
Leaders begin all decisions with humility and reverence for God to whom they are ultimately accountable.

1 Kings 12:8 *But Rehoboam rejected the advice of the elders and instead asked the opinion of the young men who had grown up with him and who were now his advisers.*
Leaders will have many people offering them advice. If you reject the advice of proven wise counselors, as Rehoboam did, you will probably make a very foolish decision. But if you listen to advice and weigh it carefully, you are more likely to make good choices.

Proverbs 18:15 *Intelligent people are always open to new ideas. In fact, they look for them.*
Leaders need to be confident in the fact that being open to good advice is not a sign of weakness or inadequacy, but of intelligence.

Matthew 16:26 *And how do you benefit if you gain the whole world but lose your own soul in the process? Is anything worth more than your soul?*
Leaders must resist the temptation to make choices guided by a desire to gain "the world"—power, prestige, fame, money. Such ambition will lead you to make some very bad decisions.

Luke 6:12-13 *One day soon afterward Jesus went to a mountain to pray, and he prayed to God all night. At daybreak he called together all of his disciples and chose twelve of them to be apostles.*
Leaders need to saturate their decisions with prayer. This is especially true in decisions concerning the selection and care for those with whom you will work most closely.

John 5:19 *Jesus replied, "I assure you, the Son can do nothing by himself. He does only what he sees the Father doing."*
If you, like Jesus, continually seek what God would have you do, then you are more likely to make good choices that honor him.

Galatians 5:22-23 *But when the Holy Spirit controls our lives, he will produce this kind of fruit in us: love, joy, peace, patience, kindness, goodness, faithfulness, gentleness, and self-control.*
Good choices are always in keeping with the fruit of the Holy Spirit, while bad choices often involve rejecting the Spirit's influence in your heart.

Psalm 25:4 *Show me the path where I should walk, O Lord; point out the right road for me to follow.*

Psalm 119:24 *Your decrees please me; they give me wise advice.*
Knowing the Scriptures and gleaning their wisdom gives you more options in your decision making and provides you with the discernment you need to make healthy choices. A right decision is consistent with the principles of truth found in God's Word.

What is the most important decision any leader can make?

Deuteronomy 30:19-20 *Oh, that you would choose life, that you and your descendants might live! Choose to love the Lord your God and to obey him and commit yourself to him, for he is your life.*

Joshua 24:15 *Choose today whom you will serve. . . . But as for me and my family, we will serve the Lord.*

John 14:6 *Jesus told him, "I am the way, the truth, and the life. No one can come to the Father except through me."*

The most important decision any leader can make is to be a follower of God. Following God and believing in his Son, Jesus, is a decision that has eternal implications.

PROMISE FROM GOD James 1:5 *If you need wisdom—if you want to know what God wants you to do—ask him, and he will gladly tell you.*

DEFEAT

See **FAILURE**

DELEGATION

See also **MENTORING**

Why is it important for leaders to delegate?

Exodus 18:14-22 *When Moses' father-in-law saw all that Moses was doing for the people, he said, "Why are you trying to do all this alone? . . . You're going to wear yourself out—and the people, too. This job is too heavy a burden for you to handle all by yourself. . . . But find some capable, honest men who fear God and hate bribes. Appoint them as judges over groups of one thousand, one hundred, fifty, and ten. These men can serve the people, resolving all the ordinary cases. Anything that is too important or too complicated can be brought to you."*

Delegation is necessary for all who are involved: for the leaders, for those who serve with the leader, and for those who are served. Without delegation, you will be over-burdened, the helpers under-utilized, and the people under-served. Delegation is not laziness, but wise stewardship of everyone's resources and time.

Ephesians 4:11-13 *He is the one who gave these gifts to the church: the apostles, the prophets, the evangelists, and the pastors and teachers. Their responsibility is to equip God's people to do his work and build up the church, the body of Christ, until we come to such unity in our faith and knowledge of God's Son that we will be mature and full grown in the Lord, measuring up to the full stature of Christ.*

Delegation is an essential part of Christian leadership. God has designed the church to be a place where everyone is involved. In fact, equipping, delegation, and involvement are the means God uses to bring all of us to maturity in Christ.

How do I delegate?

Matthew 10:1, 5 *Jesus called his twelve disciples to him and gave them authority to cast out evil spirits and to heal every kind of disease and illness. . . . Jesus sent the twelve disciples out with these instructions.*

Delegation is not simply letting go of work or "dumping" things you don't want to do on others. Delegation is a form of discipleship. After the disciples had spent some time with Jesus, he delegated his ministry in an initial way to these followers. He gave them specific instructions, trusted them, and valued their contribution.

2 Timothy 2:2 *Teach these great truths to trustworthy people who are able to pass them on to others.* Delegation develops others who, in turn, can develop others. You should care as much about helping others learn and accomplish as you care about your own accomplishments. Delegation is a primary strategy for nurturing maturity and responsibility in those you lead.

PROMISE FROM GOD 1 Corinthians 12:11 *It is the one and only Holy Spirit who distributes these gifts. He alone decides which gift each person should have.*

DEPENDENCE/DEPENDABILITY

See **RESPONSIBILITY**

DEPRESSION

See also **DISCOURAGEMENT**

How are leaders vulnerable to depression?

1 Kings 19:3-4 *Elijah was afraid and fled for his life. He went to Beersheba, a town in Judah, and he left his servant there. Then he went on alone into the desert, traveling all day. He sat down under a solitary broom tree and prayed that he might die. "I have had enough, Lord," he*

said. "Take my life, for I am no better than my ancestors."
Leaders are vulnerable to depression, especially after a major victory. Elijah had just defeated 450 prophets of Baal and seen God work several mighty miracles, yet he was afraid and depressed.

Psalm 42:3-5 *Day and night, I have only tears for food, while my enemies continually taunt me, saying, "Where is this God of yours?" My heart is breaking as I remember how it used to be: I walked among the crowds of worshipers, leading a great procession to the house of God, singing for joy and giving thanks—it was the sound of a great celebration! Why am I discouraged? Why so sad?*
Leaders often find themselves following in the aftermath of "the good old days." Such seems to be the experience of the psalmist. Depression often comes from looking backward at what you have lost.

Romans 7:15, 21 *I don't understand myself at all, for I really want to do what is right, but I don't do it. Instead, I do the very thing I hate. . . . It seems to be a fact of life that when I want to do what is right, I inevitably do what is wrong.*
A third factor in depression is the sense of loss that comes with realizing the gap between the ideal you strive for and the reality you see within and around you.

Matthew 26:36-39 *Then Jesus brought them to an olive grove called Gethsemane, and he said, "Sit here while I go on ahead to pray." He took Peter and Zebedee's two sons, James and John, and he began to be filled with anguish and deep distress. He told them, "My soul is crushed with grief to the point of death. Stay here and watch with me." He went on a little farther and fell face down on the ground, praying, "My Father! If it is possible, let this cup of suffering be taken away from me."*

While there are many other sources of depression, it can also come from being asked by God to do a very, very hard thing.

What helps leaders recover from depression?

1 Kings 19:7-15 *The angel of the Lord came again and touched him and said, "Get up and eat some more, for there is a long journey ahead of you." So he got up and ate and drank, and the food gave him enough strength to travel forty days and forty nights to Mount Sinai, the mountain of God. There he came to a cave, where he spent the night. But the Lord said to him, "What are you doing here, Elijah? . . . Go back the way you came, and travel to the wilderness of Damascus. When you arrive there, anoint Hazael to be king of Aram."*
Recovery from depression involves a number of factors, illustrated in Elijah's experience. Ruling out, of course, physiologically based depression, leaders facing depression need rest, good nutrition, and reengagement with God. Elijah was reconnected with his vision and given a fresh vision as well as specific direction for his next steps.

Psalm 42:5-8 *I will put my hope in God! I will praise him again—my Savior and my God! Now I am deeply discouraged, but I will remember your kindness. . . . I hear the tumult of the raging seas as your waves and surging tides sweep over me. Through each day the Lord pours his unfailing love upon me, and through each night I sing his songs, praying to God who gives me life.*
Leaders can resist depression by choosing hope over the lies of despair. That hope is fueled by remembering God's past faithfulness, reflecting on God's power evident all around, and meditating on spiritual truth through music and song.

Romans 7:25—8:2 *Thank God! The answer is in Jesus Christ our Lord. So you see how it is: In my mind I really want to obey God's law, but because of my sinful nature I am a slave to sin. So now there is no condemnation for those who belong to Christ Jesus. For the power of the life-giving Spirit has freed you through Christ Jesus from the power of sin that leads to death.*
You cannot solve the "ideal gap" (between the ideal you strive for and the reality of failure you experience) on your own, but Christ has solved it for you. Leaders learn to accept reality and continue to live in the hope of the gospel as it touches all of life.

Matthew 26:39-44 *"Yet I want your will, not mine." . . . Again he left them and prayed, "My Father! If this cup cannot be taken away until I drink it, your will be done." . . . So he went back to pray a third time, saying the same things again.*
When you are faced with a difficult call of God, Jesus shows that earnest, candid, repeated prayer is the way to reach the place of willing surrender. This surrender usually lifts you from depression to a joy that passes understanding.

PROMISE FROM GOD Matthew 11:28 *Then Jesus said, "Come to me, all of you who are weary and carry heavy burdens, and I will give you rest."*

DETERMINATION

See **PERSEVERANCE**

DISCERNMENT

See **DECISIONS**

DISCIPLESHIP

See **DELEGATION, MENTORING**

DISCIPLINE, CORRECTION

See **CHURCH DISCIPLINE, CONFRONTATION, PERSONAL DISCIPLINE**

DISCOURAGEMENT

See also **DEPRESSION, MOTIVATION, STRESS**

Why do leaders get discouraged?

Numbers 11:10-15 *Moses heard all the families standing in front of their tents weeping, and the Lord became extremely angry. Moses was also very aggravated. And Moses said to the Lord, "Why are you treating me, your servant, so miserably? What did I do to deserve the burden of a people like this? . . . I can't carry all these people by myself! The load is far too heavy! I'd rather you killed me than treat me like this. Please spare me this misery!"*

You can be so overwhelmed that you become almost irrational in your misery. In this case, Moses was overwhelmed by the continual demands of the people.

Psalm 55:20-21 *As for this friend of mine, he betrayed me; he broke his promises. His words are as smooth as cream, but in his heart is war. His words are as soothing as lotion, but underneath are daggers!*
You can become discouraged when people let you down. Whether it is as simple as forgetting a responsibility, or as serious as betrayal, the failure of others can make your burdens much heavier.

2 Corinthians 2:16 *And who is adequate for such a task as this?*
You may feel that you are not adequate to the task.

2 Corinthians 1:8-9 *I think you ought to know, dear brothers and sisters, about the trouble we went through in the province of Asia. We were crushed and completely overwhelmed, and we thought we would never live through it. In fact, we expected to die.*
A fourth factor in discouragement is simply the crushing burden and heartbreak of life. You often know more than you wish you did about many situations—about the real nature of people and the "dark side" of organizations. This knowledge combined with other hardships can wear you down.

How can I find hope and strength in my discouragement?

Numbers 11:16-17 *Then the Lord said to Moses, "Summon before me seventy of the leaders of Israel. Bring them to the Tabernacle to stand there with you. I will come down and talk to you there. I will take some of the Spirit that is upon you, and I will put the Spirit upon them also. They will bear the burden of the people along with you, so you will not have to carry it alone."*
The good news is that God does not rebuke you for your discouragement! Instead he responds to your

concerns with practical help, such as providing partners who can shoulder the burdens with you.

Joshua 1:9 *Be strong and courageous! Do not be afraid or discouraged. For the Lord your God is with you wherever you go.*
The greatest encouragement is to know that you only go where the Lord has already gone before you. God is always with you wherever you are.

2 Chronicles 20:15 *Don't be discouraged by this mighty army, for the battle is not yours, but God's.*
You can find strength when you remember the real battle and the real Warrior.

Psalm 119:25 *I lie in the dust, completely discouraged; revive me by your word.*
When you are overwhelmed by the needs of others, the failures of others, your own inadequacy, or the pressures of circumstances, God's Word revives you with truth that inspires faith, hope, and love.

2 Corinthians 1:9-11 *In fact, we expected to die. But as a result, we learned not to rely on ourselves, but on God who can raise the dead. And he did deliver us from mortal danger. And we are confident that he will continue to deliver us. He will rescue us because you are helping by praying for us. As a result, many will give thanks to God because so many people's prayers for our safety have been answered.*
Discouragement can teach you that you must depend on God rather than your own personality, resources, skills, or connections. You also learn to call for the prayers of others who can intercede for you.

2 Corinthians 6:4-10 *We patiently endure troubles and hardships and calamities of every kind. . . . God's power has been working in us. We have righteousness*

as our weapon, both to attack and to defend ourselves. We serve God whether people honor us or despise us, whether they slander us or praise us. . . . Our hearts ache, but we always have joy. We are poor, but we give spiritual riches to others. We own nothing, and yet we have everything.
Read this passage several times and soak in its strength, vitality, and maturity. This is whole-hearted, discouragement-resistant leadership at its best.

Psalm 34:18 *The Lord is close to the brokenhearted; he rescues those who are crushed in spirit.*

Revelation 21:4 *He will remove all of their sorrows, and there will be no more death or sorrow or crying or pain.*
God promises all you need to endure and, in the end, promises an end to all problems in the glory of eternal life.

PROMISE FROM GOD Galatians 6:9 *Don't get discouraged and give up, for we will reap a harvest of blessing at the appropriate time.*

DISHONESTY

See **CHEATING, INTEGRITY**

ELDERS

See also **DEACONS**

What are the primary characteristics of a spiritual leader?
1 Timothy 3:1-7 *It is a true saying that if someone wants to be an elder, he desires an honorable responsibility.*

For an elder must be a man whose life cannot be spoken against. He must be faithful to his wife. He must exhibit self-control, live wisely, and have a good reputation. He must enjoy having guests in his home and must be able to teach. He must not be a heavy drinker or be violent. He must be gentle, peace loving, and not one who loves money. He must manage his own family well, with children who respect and obey him. For if a man cannot manage his own household, how can he take care of God's church? An elder must not be a new Christian, because he might be proud of being chosen so soon, and the Devil will use that pride to make him fall. Also, people outside the church must speak well of him so that he will not fall into the Devil's trap and be disgraced.

Paul lists numerous characteristics for church leaders. The primary characteristic is consistency between what they believe and how they live. Leaders apply the truth of the gospel to every aspect of life. This is what is meant by "integrity"—the integration of faith and life. This can be seen in four primary areas. Leaders are maturing in (1) personal spirituality, exhibiting a vibrant faith in Jesus Christ, and ministering out of the overflow of knowing God more and more deeply; (2) emotional maturity, exercising self-control in anger, conflict, ambition, and substance use (such as alcohol and finances); (3) relational responsibility in valuing people, especially their family relationships, and being gracious hosts; and (4) ministry competency, being knowledgeable and skilled in communicating God's truth and care to others. These high standards do not mean that spiritual leaders are faultless, but that they are committed to bearing the fruit of faith in all of life.

What do elders need to watch for as leaders?

Acts 20:28-31 *And now beware! Be sure that you feed and shepherd God's flock—his church, purchased with his blood—over whom the Holy Spirit has appointed you as elders. I know full well that false teachers, like vicious wolves, will come in among you after I leave, not sparing the flock. Even some of you will distort the truth in order to draw a following. Watch out! Remember the three years I was with you—my constant watch and care over you night and day, and my many tears for you.*

Spiritual leaders are engaged in spiritual battles. In addition to the normal functions of providing for the people's welfare and direction, elders must keep watch for false teachers who threaten to seduce the people away from God's Word (2 Timothy 4:3-4). It is also interesting to note that leaders weep in concern, compassion, and love for those they lead.

1 Peter 5:1-4 *And now, a word to you who are elders in the churches. I, too, am an elder and a witness to the sufferings of Christ. And I, too, will share his glory and his honor when he returns. As a fellow elder, this is my appeal to you: Care for the flock of God entrusted to you. Watch over it willingly, not grudgingly—not for what you will get out of it, but because you are eager to serve God. Don't lord it over the people assigned to your care, but lead them by your good example. And when the head Shepherd comes, your reward will be a never-ending share in his glory and honor.*

Spiritual leaders lead selflessly, genuinely, and hopefully.

PROMISE FROM GOD Titus 1:6-7 *An elder must be well thought of for his good life. . . . An elder must live a blameless life because he is God's minister.*

EMPLOYERS/EMPLOYEES

See also **WORK**

How should an employer treat his or her employees?

Leviticus 19:13 *Always pay your hired workers promptly.*

Deuteronomy 24:14-15 *Never take advantage of poor laborers. . . . Pay them their wages. . . . Otherwise they might cry out to the Lord against you, and it would be counted against you as sin.*

James 5:4 *Hear the cries of the field workers whom you have cheated of their pay. The wages you held back cry out against you. The cries of the reapers have reached the ears of the Lord Almighty.*
Employers should always pay workers promptly and pay fair wages, because God is fair and expects fairness.

Ruth 2:4 *While she was there, Boaz arrived from Bethlehem and greeted the harvesters. "The Lord be with you!" he said. "The Lord bless you!" the harvesters replied.*
Employers should bless their workers by encouraging them and showing appreciation for what they are doing.

Ephesians 6:9 *And in the same way, you masters must treat your slaves right. Don't threaten them; remember, you both have the same Master in heaven, and he has no favorites.*
Though this passage speaks of slaves, the same principle applies to employers. Leaders should not lead through intimidation and threats, because they know that they will ultimately answer to the Lord for their own conduct.

How should an employee respond to his or her employer?

2 Kings 12:15 *No accounting was required from the construction supervisors, because they were honest and faithful workers.*

Luke 16:10 *Unless you are faithful in small matters, you won't be faithful in large ones.*

Proverbs 25:13 *Faithful messengers are as refreshing as snow in the heat of summer. They revive the spirit of their employer.*
Employees should be completely faithful and honest in their work.

Proverbs 10:26 *Lazy people are a pain to their employer. They are like smoke in the eyes or vinegar that sets the teeth on edge.*
Employees should work hard for their employers.

Ecclesiastes 10:4 *If your boss is angry with you, don't quit! A quiet spirit can overcome even great mistakes.*
Even if an employer is critical and overbearing, the employee should continue to do his or her best and please God.

Luke 3:14 *"What should we do?" asked some soldiers. John replied, "Don't extort money, and . . . be content with your pay."*
Employees should learn to be content with their wages and not try to get more by cheating.

Colossians 3:22-23 *You slaves must obey your earthly masters in everything you do. Try to please them all the time, not just when they are watching you. Obey them willingly because of your reverent fear of the Lord. Work hard and cheerfully at whatever you do, as though you were working for the Lord rather than for people.*

Though this passage speaks in terms of slaves and their masters, the principles apply to all work settings.

PROMISE FROM GOD Proverbs 27:18 *Workers who protect their employer's interests will be rewarded.*

ENCOURAGEMENT

Why is it necessary for me to encourage those I lead?

1 Samuel 23:16 *Jonathan went to find David and encouraged him to stay strong in his faith in God.*
Leaders know that those who are struggling need the strength that comes from compassion and encouragement.

1 Thessalonians 5:14 *Encourage those who are timid. Take tender care of those who are weak. Be patient with everyone.*
Leaders can best motivate by encouragement, not embarrassment.

Hebrews 10:24 *Think of ways to encourage one another to outbursts of love and good deeds.*
Encouragement usually inspires people not only to do their best, but also to be gracious, loving, and encouraging to others.

2 Corinthians 13:11 *Dear brothers and sisters, I close my letter with these last words: Rejoice. Change your ways. Encourage each other. Live in harmony and peace. Then the God of love and peace will be with you.*
Encouragement helps to create a relational environment where God's Spirit can move easily among and through us.

How do I communicate encouragement?

Matthew 3:16-17 *After his baptism, as Jesus came up out of the water, the heavens were opened and he saw the Spirit of God descending like a dove and settling on him. And a voice from heaven said, "This is my beloved Son, and I am fully pleased with him."*

Matthew 17:5 *A voice from the cloud said, "This is my beloved Son, and I am fully pleased with him. Listen to him."*

You communicate how you value those you lead through open affirmation and encouragement. The most vivid example of this is God's affirmation of Jesus at his baptism and transfiguration.

1 Thessalonians 5:11 *So encourage each other and build each other up, just as you are already doing.*

Ephesians 4:29 *Don't use foul or abusive language. Let everything you say be good and helpful, so that your words will be an encouragement to those who hear them.*

Words can foster or hinder encouragement. You provide an atmosphere of encouragement by setting a verbal tone that communicates harmony and peace.

Colossians 3:16 *Let the words of Christ, in all their richness, live in your hearts and make you wise. Use his words to teach and counsel each other. Sing psalms and hymns and spiritual songs to God with thankful hearts.*

Titus 1:9 *He must have a strong and steadfast belief in the trustworthy message he was taught; then he will be able to encourage others with right teaching and show those who oppose it where they are wrong.*

Your encouragement of others is rooted in the encouragement you find in God's Word.

2 Chronicles 30:22 *Hezekiah encouraged the Levites for the skill they displayed as they served the Lord.*
You can build others up by acknowledging their quality service to the Lord.

Job 29:24 *When they were discouraged, I smiled at them. My look of approval was precious to them.*

Proverbs 15:30 *A cheerful look brings joy to the heart; good news makes for good health.*
You can encourage others simply with a joyful spirit.

2 Chronicles 32:8 *"He may have a great army, but they are just men. We have the Lord our God to help us and to fight our battles for us!" These words greatly encouraged the people.*
You can encourage by reminding people what God can do and wants to do for and through them.

Acts 11:23 *[Barnabas] encouraged the believers to stay true to the Lord.*
Barnabas is known as the "great encourager" in the Bible. Barnabas's encouragement of John Mark helped him become a great leader in the church. Encouragement is more than hollow praise; it is urging others to hold fast to the principles of faith.

Philippians 1:6 *And I am sure that God, who began the good work within you, will continue his work until it is finally finished.*
You can encourage others by affirming the work they are doing for God.

PROMISE FROM GOD Joshua 23:10 *Each one of you will put to flight a thousand of the enemy, for the Lord your God fights for you, just as he has promised.*

ENDURANCE

See **PERSEVERANCE**

ENVY

See also **COMPETITION, JEALOUSY**

How do leaders struggle with envy?

Genesis 26:12, 14 *That year Isaac's crops were tremendous! . . . Soon the Philistines became jealous of him.*

James 4:2 *You want what you don't have, so you scheme and kill to get it. You are jealous for what others have, and you can't possess it, so you fight and quarrel to take it away from them.*
Envy is primarily desiring what you don't have and jealousy is primarily possessiveness and the fear of losing what you do have (though the words are often used interchangeably). You can find yourself dissatisfied with your situation and envying (or longing for in an unhealthy way) the success others currently seem to be enjoying.

Daniel 6:3-4 *Daniel soon proved himself more capable than all the other administrators and princes. Because of his great ability, the king made plans to place him over the entire empire. Then the other administrators and princes began searching for some fault in the way Daniel was handling his affairs.*
You may find yourself the subject of another's envy when that other person sees you doing a better job.

What is the result of envy?

Job 5:2 *Surely resentment destroys the fool, and jealousy kills the simple.*

Proverbs 14:30 *A relaxed attitude lengthens life; jealousy rots it away.*

Proverbs 27:4 *Anger is cruel, and wrath is like a flood, but who can survive the destructiveness of jealousy?*

James 3:16 *For wherever there is jealousy and selfish ambition, there you will find disorder and every kind of evil.*
Envy and jealousy unchecked will eventually destroy you.

How can I control envious feelings?

Psalm 73:3, 16-20 *For I envied the proud when I saw them prosper despite their wickedness. . . . So I tried to understand why the wicked prosper. But what a difficult task it is! Then one day I went into your sanctuary, O God, and I thought about the destiny of the wicked. . . . In an instant they are destroyed, swept away by terrors. Their present life is only a dream that is gone when they awake.*

Psalm 37:1, 7 *Don't worry about the wicked. Don't envy those who do wrong. . . . Be still in the presence of the Lord, and wait patiently for him to act.*

Proverbs 24:19-20 *Do not fret because of evildoers; don't envy the wicked. For the evil have no future; their light will be snuffed out.*
It is foolish to envy the wicked who prosper, because their prosperity is only temporary. You should appreciate what God provides and accept where God calls you. Rather than simply trying to get what you don't have or allowing bitterness to take hold in your life, patiently wait for God to act in the way that is best for you.

Ecclesiastes 4:4 *Then I observed that most people are motivated to success by their envy of their neighbors. But this, too, is meaningless, like chasing the wind.*
True motivation comes from within as you seek to please the Lord, not from the envy that arises from comparison and competition with others.

John 21:20-22 *Peter turned around and saw the disciple Jesus loved following them. . . . Peter asked Jesus, "What about him, Lord?" Jesus replied, "If I want him to remain alive until I return, what is that to you? You follow me."*
Pay attention to the Lord and to yourself. You have been given a unique role to fulfill. Rather than worrying about others' position or advantages, trust God to work out his plan for you.

PROMISE FROM GOD Psalm 37:8 *Do not envy others—it only leads to harm.*

ETERNITY

Why does a wise leader need an eternal perspective?
Mark 8:36-37 *And how do you benefit if you gain the whole world but lose your own soul in the process? Is anything worth more than your soul?*

Luke 12:15, 21 *Then he said, "Beware! Don't be greedy for what you don't have. Real life is not measured by how much we own." . . . A person is a fool to store up earthly wealth but not have a rich relationship with God."*
So much of what leaders are tempted to pursue on a daily basis has little or no eternal value. Leaders must remind others of eternal priorities. This will help you keep all things in proper perspective. You won't be too

elated when earthly things go well, nor too distressed if they fail.

PROMISE FROM GOD Matthew 16:25 *If you try to keep your life for yourself, you will lose it. But if you give up your life for me, you will find true life.*

ETHICS

See **INTEGRITY**

EVALUATION

Why is it necessary for leaders to evaluate their organization or group?

Exodus 39:42-43 *So the people of Israel followed all of the Lord's instructions to Moses. Moses inspected all their work and blessed them because it had been done as the Lord had commanded him.*

Evaluation and inspection are an essential part of success. You need to hold your organization or group accountable to being evaluated so that there are objective criteria for growth, productivity, and quality. Leaders keep the organization asking the right questions and assessing their work. In addition, you have the difficult task of examining people to determine their fitness for particular tasks and responsibilities. This may seem like judging a person, but it isn't. Judging has to do with reaching a negative conclusion about a person's eternal destiny—something only God can know. Evaluation is about determining a person's fitness for service and for discerning areas for growth and development.

PROMISE FROM GOD 1 Peter 4:10 *God has given gifts to each of you from his great variety of spiritual gifts. Manage them well so that God's generosity can flow through you.*

EVANGELISM

What does evangelism have to do with leadership?
1 Peter 2:12 *Be careful how you live among your unbelieving neighbors. Even if they accuse you of doing wrong, they will see your honorable behavior, and they will believe and give honor to God when he comes to judge the world.*
Leaders understand that the ultimate goal of life is to be in relationship with God. Keep this in mind as you work with people who don't know the Lord. Don't abuse your position of power to coerce commitment, but do use opportunities to encourage those you lead to consider the "big picture" of life.

Matthew 5:13-16 *You are the salt of the earth. . . . You are the light of the world—like a city on a mountain, glowing in the night for all to see. Don't hide your light under a basket! Instead, put it on a stand and let it shine for all. In the same way, let your good deeds shine out for all to see, so that everyone will praise your heavenly Father.*
Responsible Christian lifestyle is a witness to others. The way you live should praise the Lord and attract others to him.

PROMISE FROM GOD Luke 12:8 *If anyone acknowledges me publicly here on earth, I, the Son of Man, will openly acknowledge that person in the presence of God's angels.*

EXCELLENCE

Why should leaders seek excellence?

Genesis 1:31 *Then God looked over all he had made, and he saw that it was excellent in every way.*
The creation God made was excellent in every way. The glory of the Creator was reflected in the glory of his creation. That is the highest standard of excellence.

How can I encourage the pursuit of excellence?

Exodus 35:31 *The Lord has filled Bezalel with . . . skill in all kinds of crafts.*
Recognize the people God has gifted for particular service and encourage them to use their gifts.

1 Chronicles 26:6 *Shemaiah had sons with great ability who earned positions of great authority.*
Value those who perform with excellence and promote them to significant positions.

Nehemiah 13:13 *These men had an excellent reputation, and it was their job to make honest distributions to their fellow Levites.*
Trust people who have an excellent reputation and entrust them with high responsibilities.

PROMISE FROM GOD Colossians 3:23-24 *Work hard and cheerfully at whatever you do, as though you were working for the Lord rather than for people. Remember that the Lord will give you an inheritance as your reward, and the Master you are serving is Christ.*

FAILURE

How are leaders to respond to failure?

Joshua 7:7 *Then Joshua cried out, "Sovereign Lord, why did you bring us across the Jordan River if you are going to let the Amorites kill us?"*

Initially, leaders may not understand the true cause of failure. In this situation, Joshua brought the defeat before the Lord in prayer and learned that the true source of the failure was Achan's unfaithfulness. Seek God's direction and good counsel in assessing and responding to failure.

Proverbs 24:16 *They may trip seven times, but each time they will rise again. But one calamity is enough to lay the wicked low.*

Micah 7:8 *Though I fall, I will rise again. Though I sit in darkness, the Lord himself will be my light.*

The best response to failure is to get up again, with the help and hope that faith in God brings.

Psalm 37:23-24 *The steps of the godly are directed by the Lord. He delights in every detail of their lives. Though they stumble, they will not fall, for the Lord holds them by the hand.*

Leaders should demonstrate resilience in failure, trusting the Lord to sustain them.

PROMISE FROM GOD Hebrews 13:5 *For God has said, "I will never fail you. I will never forsake you."*

FAIRNESS

See also **JUSTICE**

In what ways can I treat others fairly?

Exodus 23:2-3 *When you are on the witness stand, do not be swayed in your testimony by the opinion of the majority. And do not slant your testimony in favor of a person just because that person is poor.*

Leviticus 19:15 *Always judge your neighbors fairly, neither favoring the poor nor showing deference to the rich.*

James 2:8-9 *Yes indeed, it is good when you truly obey our Lord's royal command found in the Scriptures: "Love your neighbor as yourself." But if you pay special attention to the rich, you are committing a sin, for you are guilty of breaking that law.*
Do not show favoritism. Evaluate and treat others fairly.

Isaiah 33:15 *The ones who can live here are those who are honest and fair, who reject making a profit by fraud, who stay far away from bribes, who refuse to listen to those who plot murder, who shut their eyes to all enticement to do wrong.*
Work for justice and fairness for others.

Zechariah 8:16 *But this is what you must do: Tell the truth to each other. Render verdicts in your courts that are just and that lead to peace.*
In truthfulness and fairness, recognize the other person as an equal.

How should I respond when life isn't fair?

Ezekiel 18:25 *Yet you say, "The Lord isn't being just!" Listen to me, O people of Israel. Am I the one who is unjust, or is it you?*

You need to help yourself and those you lead to not blame God for the unfairness of other people.

Ecclesiastes 9:11 *The fastest runner doesn't always win the race, and the strongest warrior doesn't always win the battle. The wise are often poor, and the skillful are not necessarily wealthy.*
Fairness is not the same as equality. God doesn't give us all the same circumstances, the same job, the same kind of family, the same environment in which to live. Since we are all unique individuals, he treats us differently in order to bring each of us to him. But he loves us all the same and desires the same salvation for us all.

Isaiah 9:7 *His ever expanding, peaceful government will never end. He will rule forever with fairness and justice.*
Recognize that God will ultimately triumph with justice and fairness.

Psalm 37:28 *The Lord loves justice, and he will never abandon the godly. He will keep them safe forever.*
Remember that your ultimate hope for vindication is in your Lord alone.

PROMISE FROM GOD Jeremiah 22:3-4 *This is what the Lord says: Be fair-minded and just. Do what is right! . . . If you obey me, there will always be a descendant of David sitting on the throne.*

FAITHFULNESS

See also **LOYALTY**

How is faithfulness significant to leaders?

1 Corinthians 4:2 *Now, a person who is put in charge as a manager must be faithful.*

Nehemiah 7:2 *I gave the responsibility of governing Jerusalem to my brother Hanani, along with Hananiah, the commander of the fortress, for he was a faithful man who feared God more than most.*
Faithfulness, or trustworthiness, is essential for all who are in positions of responsibility where others are depending on them.

How do I develop faithfulness?

2 Kings 12:15 *No accounting was required from the construction supervisors, because they were honest and faithful workers.*

Daniel 6:4 *But they couldn't find anything to criticize. He was faithful and honest.*
Honesty and integrity in the everyday choices and responsibilities of life cultivate the holy habit of faithfulness.

Proverbs 3:3-4 *Never let loyalty and kindness get away from you! . . . Then you will . . . gain a good reputation.*
Loyalty and kindness are marks of a leader who has the welfare of others as a top priority. Such faithfulness brings a good reputation and trust from others.

What are the rewards of faithfulness?

2 Samuel 22:25-27 *The Lord rewarded me for doing right, because of my innocence in his sight. To the*

faithful you show yourself faithful; to those with integrity you show integrity. To the pure you show yourself pure, but to the wicked you show yourself hostile.
Faithful leaders know God more deeply and experience the grace of God's faithfulness.

Luke 19:17 *You have been faithful with the little I have entrusted to you, so you will be governor of ten cities as your reward.*
Faithfulness in small things brings greater opportunities.

Numbers 14:24 *My servant Caleb is different from the others. He has remained loyal to me, and I will bring him into the land he explored. His descendants will receive their full share of that land.*
Faithfulness to God will be rewarded with blessings for you and for your descendants.

Proverbs 2:8 *He guards the paths of justice and protects those who are faithful to him.*
God watches out for those who honor him by living faithfully.

Hebrews 3:14 *If we are faithful to the end, . . . we will share in all that belongs to Christ.*

Revelation 2:10 *Remain faithful even when facing death, and I will give you the crown of life.*
Heavenly rewards await those who are faithful to God.

PROMISES FROM GOD Deuteronomy 7:9 *He is the faithful God who keeps his covenant for a thousand generations.*

2 Thessalonians 3:3 *But the Lord is faithful; he will make you strong and guard you from the evil one.*

FAME

See **REPUTATION**

FAMILY

Why should leaders care about their families?

1 Samuel 2:12-13, 22, 25 *Now the sons of Eli were scoundrels who had no respect for the Lord or for their duties as priests. . . . Now Eli was very old, but he was aware of what his sons were doing to the people of Israel. . . . But Eli's sons wouldn't listen to their father.*
Your family can cause great help or great harm to you and to the larger community.

1 Kings 1:6 *Now [Adonijah's] father, King David, had never disciplined him at any time, even by asking, "What are you doing?"*
Your failure to discipline your children can threaten your own plans. David's failure led his son, Adonijah, to try to establish himself as king in place of Solomon.

1 Timothy 3:4-5 *He must manage his own family well, with children who respect and obey him. For if a man cannot manage his own household, how can he take care of God's church?*
The way you lead your family reveals a great deal about your ability to lead others.

1 Timothy 5:8 *But those who won't care for their own relatives, especially those living in the same household, have denied what we believe. Such people are worse than unbelievers.*
Leadership in all its aspects begins at home.

PROMISE FROM GOD Deuteronomy 6:5-7
And you must love the Lord your God with all your heart, all your soul, and all your strength. And you must commit yourselves wholeheartedly to these commands I am giving you today. Repeat them again and again to your children. Talk about them when you are at home and when you are away on a journey, when you are lying down and when you are getting up again.

FATIGUE

See **BURNOUT, SABBATH**

FLATTERY

See also **PRIDE**

How are leaders vulnerable to flattery?

Proverbs 29:5 *To flatter people is to lay a trap for their feet.*
You can be vulnerable to flattery because you are likely to be the object of attention. Flattery is a dangerous trap because it is manipulative. Flattery may disguise anger, ambition, or any number of unhealthy motives that undermine a relationship.

Proverbs 7:21-23 *She seduced him with her pretty speech. With her flattery she enticed him. He followed her at once. . . . He was like a bird flying into a snare, little knowing it would cost him his life.*
In its most dishonest and deceptive form, flattery is a lie that leads into sin. Leaders, male and female, must beware of the flattery that can lead to sexual compromise.

How should I view flattery?
1 Thessalonians 2:5 *Never once did we try to win you with flattery.*
Refuse to use flattery as a manipulative tool to accomplish your goals. Speak the truth in love (Ephesians 4:15).

PROMISE FROM GOD Proverbs 26:28 *A lying tongue hates its victims, and flattery causes ruin.*

FOCUS

See **GOALS**

FORGIVENESS

See also **CONFLICT, BETRAYAL**

Why are leaders concerned with forgiveness?
Colossians 3:13 *You must make allowance for each other's faults and forgive the person who offends you. Remember, the Lord forgave you, so you must forgive others.*

Matthew 6:14-15 *If you forgive those who sin against you, your heavenly Father will forgive you. But if you refuse to forgive others, your Father will not forgive your sins.*
The stress and tensions of leadership and community mean there will be frequent conflicts and problems between leaders and those they lead. Wise leaders make candid confession and forgiveness a way of life for their group or organization. You must set the tone with believers and nonbelievers alike. Be motivated by

the clear teaching of God's Word that you will receive God's forgiveness only when you are willing to forgive others who have wronged you.

Matthew 18:21-22 *Peter came to him and asked, "Lord, how often should I forgive someone who sins against me? Seven times?" "No!" Jesus replied, "seventy times seven!"*
Just as God forgives without limit, so you should forgive others without counting how many times.

2 Corinthians 2:5-8 *I am not overstating it when I say that the man who caused all the trouble hurt your entire church more than he hurt me. He was punished enough when most of you were united in your judgment against him. Now it is time to forgive him and comfort him. Otherwise he may become so discouraged that he won't be able to recover. Now show him that you still love him.*
Leaders understand that refusing to forgive a person can lead to serious harmful consequences for the offender. It is acceptable to require a person to suffer natural and logical consequences for mistakes or offenses, but do not discourage him or her by withholding forgiveness.

How can I forgive those who have hurt me deeply?
Luke 23:34 *Jesus said, "Father, forgive these people, because they don't know what they are doing."*
Jesus forgave those who mocked and killed him. You need to think more of the people involved and of your own relationship with God than you do of nursing your grudges and self-pity.

PROMISE FROM GOD Isaiah 1:18 *No matter how deep the stain of your sins, I can remove it. I can make you as clean as freshly fallen snow.*

FRIENDS

See **RELATIONSHIPS**

FRUSTRATION

Why do leaders anticipate frustration?

Genesis 3:17-19 *I have placed a curse on the ground. All your life you will struggle to scratch a living from it. It will grow thorns and thistles for you, though you will eat of its grains. All your life you will sweat to produce food, until your dying day.*

Frustration is the consequence of the curse of sin. While we do not welcome it, we are not surprised by it. We live in a fallen world with fallen people; therefore leaders must expect obstacles and resistance in all forms. When you anticipate frustration and difficulty at times in your leadership position, you are better prepared mentally to handle it in a godly, redemptive way.

How can I best deal with frustration?

Ecclesiastes 1:8 *Everything is so weary and tiresome! No matter how much we see, we are never satisfied. No matter how much we hear, we are not content.*

Acts 17:25 *Human hands can't serve his needs—for he has no needs. He himself gives life and breath to everything, and he satisfies every need there is.*

You may be frustrated when you fail to let God be God, or when you try to understand the reasons for everything that happens. When you let go and trust God to work out what is best for you, you will relieve much of your frustration.

PROMISE FROM GOD Joshua 1:9 *I command you—be strong and courageous! Do not be afraid or discouraged. For the Lord your God is with you wherever you go.*

GIVING

See **STEWARDSHIP**

GOALS

See also **MOTIVATION, VISION**

Why are goals important for leaders?

Genesis 12:1-3 *Then the Lord told Abram, "Leave your country, your relatives, and your father's house, and go to the land that I will show you. I will cause you to become the father of a great nation. I will bless you and make you famous, and I will make you a blessing to others. I will bless those who bless you and curse those who curse you. All the families of the earth will be blessed through you."*
God's goals set the agenda for our lives. God's promise to Abram gave him such a strong purpose and direction that he was willing to risk everything on it.

1 Chronicles 22:5 *David said, "My son Solomon is still young and inexperienced, and the Temple of the Lord must be a magnificent structure, famous and glorious throughout the world. So I will begin making preparations for it now." So David collected vast amounts of building materials before his death.*
A bold vision can help the leader and people accomplish great goals. David's vision for the Temple was fulfilled in the construction of a magnificent structure for the glory of God.

Mark 10:45 *For even I, the Son of Man, came here not to be served but to serve others, and to give my life as a ransom for many.*
A goal keeps you focused on your primary mission and determines how you conduct your life. Jesus' goal of giving his life shaped the way he lived every day, guiding every interaction with others.

John 17:4 *I brought glory to you here on earth by doing everything you told me to do.*
Leaders are often tempted to do too much. But God gives you only what you can accomplish by living a godly, balanced life. God is glorified not by your doing everything you can possibly do, but rather by your fulfilling the goals he has for you.

How should I pursue my goals?

Matthew 28:19-20 *Therefore, go and make disciples of all the nations, baptizing them in the name of the Father and the Son and the Holy Spirit. Teach these new disciples to obey all the commands I have given you. And be sure of this: I am with you always, even to the end of the age.*
No matter what you do as a leader, Jesus' ultimate goal for all his followers is sharing the good news with all people, everywhere.

Romans 15:20-21 *My ambition has always been to preach the Good News where the name of Christ has never been heard, rather than where a church has already been started by someone else. I have been following the plan spoken of in the Scriptures, where it says, "Those who have never been told about him will see, and those who have never heard of him will understand."*
Continue to have goals that carry you through life. Paul was an older man when he wrote this, but he was

still driven by his goal to take the gospel message as far as Spain.

Philippians 3:13-14 *I am focusing all my energies on this one thing: Forgetting the past and looking forward to what lies ahead, I strain to reach the end of the race and receive the prize for which God, through Christ Jesus, is calling us up to heaven.*

1 Corinthians 9:26 *I run straight to the goal with purpose in every step. I am not like a boxer who misses his punches.*
Keep your eyes on the target, resisting temptations to get sidetracked. Stay focused on your primary goal in order to be most effective and make the most significant progress and impact.

1 Corinthians 14:1 *Let love be your highest goal.*
Make it your goal to foster harmony and love with other Christians.

James 4:4 *If your aim is to enjoy this world, you can't be a friend of God.*

2 Corinthians 5:9 *So our aim is to please him always.*
Whatever you do, your goal should be to please God, not the world.

PROMISE FROM GOD Psalm 37:4 *Take delight in the Lord, and he will give you your heart's desires.*

GOD'S WILL

See also **CALL OF GOD/CALLING**

Why is discerning God's will important for a leader?

Matthew 6:9-10 *Pray like this: Our Father in heaven, may your name be honored. May your Kingdom come soon. May your will be done here on earth, just as it is in heaven.*

If the accomplishment of God's will is the first priority of prayer, it must be the first priority of leaders.

Acts 16:7-10 *Then coming to the borders of Mysia, they headed for the province of Bithynia, but again the Spirit of Jesus did not let them go. So instead, they went on through Mysia to the city of Troas. That night Paul had a vision. He saw a man from Macedonia in northern Greece, pleading with him, "Come over here and help us." So we decided to leave for Macedonia at once, for we could only conclude that God was calling us to preach the Good News there.*

Leaders often face far too many opportunities. Discerning God's will helps you recognize the best opportunities in the midst of the good ones, and the ones with the most potential in the midst of the innumerable possibilities.

Does God really have a plan for my life?

Psalm 139:3 *You chart the path ahead of me and tell me where to stop and rest. Every moment you know where I am.*

You can learn the value of every moment because God cares about even the seemingly smallest details of your life. In fact, God's love is seen in his care in the small things.

Philippians 1:6 *And I am sure that God, who began the good work within you, will continue his work until it is finally finished on that day when Christ Jesus comes back again.*

Psalm 138:8 *The Lord will work out his plans for my life.*
When facing frustrations and setbacks, you can rest assured that God's will accomplish his plans for you.

Psalm 32:8 *The Lord says, "I will guide you along the best pathway for your life. I will advise you and watch over you."*
God definitely wants to help you follow the path that will be most pleasing to him, not the path that may be most pleasing to you.

What are some things I should do to discover God's will?
Proverbs 2:3-5 *Cry out for insight and understanding. Search for them as you would for lost money or hidden treasure. Then you will understand what it means to fear the Lord.*

Matthew 7:7-8 *Keep on asking, and you will be given what you ask for. Keep on looking, and you will find. Keep on knocking, and the door will be opened. For everyone who asks, receives. Everyone who seeks, finds. And the door is opened to everyone who knocks.*

1 John 5:14 *And we can be confident that he will listen to us whenever we ask him for anything in line with his will.*
Actively seek God's will through prayer, through conversation with mature believers and reliable advisers, and by discerning the circumstances around you.

Isaiah 2:3 *Come, let us go up to the mountain of the Lord, to the Temple of the God of Israel. There he will teach us his ways, so that we may obey them.*
Let God direct you through his Word.

James 1:5 *If you want to know what God wants you to do—ask him, and he will gladly tell you. He will not resent your asking.*
Sometimes the best way to know God's will is to let go and let God have his wonderful way. You may learn more about his will as you allow him to work out his will in your life.

Proverbs 16:3 *Commit your work to the Lord, and then your plans will succeed.*
God's will is that you do everything as if you were doing it for him.

PROMISE FROM GOD Proverbs 3:6 *Seek his will in all you do, and he will direct your paths.*

GREATNESS

See also **HUMILITY, SERVANTHOOD**

How is greatness measured?
1 Corinthians 1:26-29 *Remember, dear brothers and sisters, that few of you were wise in the world's eyes, or powerful, or wealthy when God called you. Instead, God deliberately chose things the world considers foolish in order to shame those who think they are wise. And he chose those who are powerless to shame those who are powerful. God chose things despised by the world, things counted as nothing at all, and used them to bring to nothing what the world considers important, so that no one can ever boast in the presence of God.*

Greatness is measured in ways that this world often misses. For leaders this means that you adjust your expectations to God's criteria.

How does a Christian understanding of greatness affect my choices and behavior as a leader?

Mark 9:33-35 *Jesus asked them, "What were you discussing out on the road?" But they didn't answer, because they had been arguing about which of them was the greatest. He sat down and called the twelve disciples over to him. Then he said, "Anyone who wants to be the first must take last place and be the servant of everyone else."*

1 Samuel 18:3-4 *And Jonathan made a special vow to be David's friend, and he sealed the pact by giving him his robe, tunic, sword, bow, and belt.*

If you measure yourself or others by worldly standards of greatness, you will miss God's will for you and your situation. Jonathan, Saul's son, was heir apparent to Israel's throne, but that didn't blind him to God's plan. We see Jonathan's greatness in the fact that he recognized and responded to the fact that God was giving the throne to David. Jesus said the first shall be last and the last first. This "great reversal" fools many who buy into the world's system.

PROMISE FROM GOD Luke 9:48 *Then he said to them, "Anyone who welcomes a little child like this on my behalf welcomes me, and anyone who welcomes me welcomes my Father who sent me. Whoever is the least among you is the greatest."*

GREED

See also **MONEY**

What does greed do to leaders?

Proverbs 21:26 *They are always greedy for more, while the godly love to give!*

Isaiah 56:11 *And they are as greedy as dogs, never satisfied, . . . all of them intent on personal gain.*
Greed undermines and ruins leaders. Instead of keeping the welfare of those they lead and serve, greedy leaders ignore others' needs and think only of themselves.

1 Corinthians 5:11 *You are not to associate with anyone who claims to be a Christian yet indulges in sexual sin, or is greedy.*
In this passage, God ranks greed with some of the worst kinds of sin.

Proverbs 11:24 *But those who are stingy will lose everything.*
Leaders who insist on having it all often wind up with little or nothing. The more a leader accumulates through greed, the greater the chances of losing everything.

How can I resist the temptation of greed?

Matthew 6:19-21 *Don't store up treasures here on earth. . . . Store your treasures in heaven. . . . Wherever your treasure is, there your heart and thoughts will also be.*
Leaders keep the eternal perspective. Actively invest in things that will last, not in temporal treasures.

PROMISE FROM GOD Proverbs 1:19 *Such is the fate of all who are greedy for gain. It ends up robbing them of life.*

GUIDANCE

See **GOD'S WILL**

HONESTY

See **INTEGRITY**

HOSPITALITY

How are leaders called to hospitality?

Mark 10:45 *For even I, the Son of Man, came here not to be served but to serve others.*

Luke 9:12-13 *Late in the afternoon the twelve disciples came to him and said, "Send the crowds away to the nearby villages and farms, so they can find food and lodging for the night. There is nothing to eat here in this deserted place." But Jesus said, "You feed them."*

Leaders can enrich their leadership by seeing it in terms of hospitality. There are two types of people in the world—those who see themselves as guests who should be taken care of and those who see themselves as hosts who will serve and care for others. Leaders are the hosts who seek the welfare of those in their group or organization.

PROMISES FROM GOD Hebrews 13:2 *Don't forget to show hospitality to strangers, for some who have done this have entertained angels without realizing it!*

Matthew 25:35-40 *"I was hungry, and you fed me. I was thirsty, and you gave me a drink. . . . I was sick, and you cared for me." . . . And the King will tell them, "I assure you, when you did it to one of the least of these my brothers and sisters, you were doing it to me!"*

HUMILITY

See also **GREATNESS, PRIDE, SERVANTHOOD**

How does humility help my understanding of leadership?

John 3:27-30 *John replied, "God in heaven appoints each person's work. You yourselves know how plainly I told you that I am not the Messiah. . . . He must become greater and greater, and I must become less and less."*
Understand that your leadership is "appointed by God," not earned by your own efforts. While you are responsible in your work, don't be prideful. John the Baptist, whom Jesus called the greatest on earth, humbled himself so that he could lift up Jesus.

Philippians 2:5-8 *Your attitude should be the same that Christ Jesus had. Though he was God, he did not demand and cling to his rights as God. He made himself nothing; he took the humble position of a slave and appeared in human form. And in human form he obediently humbled himself even further by dying a criminal's death on a cross.*
Do not cling to your prerogatives as a means for self-advancement. Instead use your gifts, responsibilities, and resources for service and sacrifice.

Matthew 11:29 *Take my yoke upon you. Let me teach you, because I am humble and gentle, and you will find rest for your souls.*
Be accessible. Jesus is the ultimate role model of a

leader who communicated availability through gentleness and humility.

Matthew 6:1 *Take care! Don't do your good deeds publicly, to be admired, because then you will lose the reward from your Father in heaven.*

Acts 20:19 *I have done the Lord's work humbly—yes, and with tears.*
Leaders are often tempted to be proud of their work in an unhealthy way. While it is acceptable to take satisfaction in what you do, don't give in to pride.

How can humility help me when I face hard times in leadership?
Numbers 12:1-3 *While they were at Hazeroth, Miriam and Aaron criticized Moses. . . . But the Lord heard them. Now Moses was more humble than any other person on earth.*
Leaders find strength and vindication in humility. Meekness and humility are not weakness. Humility allows you to trust your reputation to the Lord.

1 Peter 5:5-7 *"God sets himself against the proud, but he shows favor to the humble." So humble yourselves under the mighty power of God, and in his good time he will honor you. Give all your worries and cares to God, for he cares about what happens to you.*
Pride can keep you from seeking the help you need. Wise leaders admit their need in any and all situations. Remember that God cares about you and will help you.

How does God respond to the humble?
Psalm 25:9 *He leads the humble in what is right, teaching them his way.*
God leads and teaches the humble.

Psalm 149:4 *For the Lord delights in his people; he crowns the humble with salvation.*
The Lord takes delight in the humble and offers them salvation.

Daniel 10:12 *Then he said, "Don't be afraid, Daniel. Since the first day you began to pray for understanding and to humble yourself before your God, your request has been heard in heaven. I have come in answer to your prayer."*
God acknowledges the prayers of the humble.

Isaiah 57:15 *I refresh the humble.*
God gives joy and refreshment to the humble.

Psalm 138:6 *Though the Lord is great, he cares for the humble, but he keeps his distance from the proud.*
God takes care of the humble.

Psalm 147:6 *The Lord supports the humble, but he brings the wicked down into the dust.*
God supports the humble.

PROMISE FROM GOD Matthew 23:12 *But those who exalt themselves will be humbled, and those who humble themselves will be exalted.*

HYPOCRISY

See also **CHARACTER**

How does hypocrisy hurt a leader?

1 Samuel 13:11-12 *But Samuel said, "What is this you have done?" Saul replied, "I saw my men scattering from me, and you didn't arrive when you said you would, and the Philistines are at Micmash ready for battle. So I*

said, 'The Philistines are ready to march against us, and I haven't even asked for the Lord's help!' So I felt obliged to offer the burnt offering myself before you came."
Hypocrisy can cost you everything. Saul was rejected as king because of his hypocrisy. He claimed to value God, but was simply watching out for himself. A wise leader is genuine.

1 Samuel 24:16-22 *Saul called back, "Is that really you, my son David? . . . May the Lord reward you well for the kindness you have shown me today." . . . But David and his men went back to their stronghold.*
Hypocrisy can cost you your credibility and your relationships of trust with others. Saul's apparent contrition did not convince David. He returned instead to a safe place far from Saul. A wise leader realizes that what might be gained by hypocrisy will be lost in credibility.

Acts 19:15-16 *But when they tried it on a man possessed by an evil spirit, the spirit replied, "I know Jesus, and I know Paul. But who are you?" And he leaped on them and attacked them with such violence that they fled from the house, naked and badly injured.*
Hypocrites try the latest formula without having an authentic commitment. The seven sons of Sceva, Jewish exorcists, tried to cast out demons in Jesus' name without having genuine faith in Jesus—and paid for it dearly. A wise leader leads out of heart commitments.

PROMISE FROM GOD Ezekiel 14:10 *False prophets and hypocrites—evil people who claim to want my advice—will all be punished for their sins.*

INTEGRITY

See also **CHARACTER, CHEATING, PROMISES, TEMPTATION**

What is integrity?

Psalm 15:1-2 *Who may worship in your sanctuary, Lord? Who may enter your presence on your holy hill? Those who lead blameless lives and do what is right, speaking the truth from sincere hearts.*
Integrity means living a life that is consistent in belief and behavior, in words and deeds. Your integrity is reflected in your relationships with God and with other people.

Job 2:3 *Then the Lord asked Satan, "Have you noticed my servant Job? He is the finest man in all the earth—a man of complete integrity. He fears God and will have nothing to do with evil. And he has maintained his integrity, even though you persuaded me to harm him without cause."*
Integrity means having beliefs, character, and conduct that are in harmony with God.

Proverbs 11:3, 5 *Good people are guided by their honesty; treacherous people are destroyed by their dishonesty. . . . The godly are directed by their honesty; the wicked fall beneath their load of sin.*
Integrity is the guiding principle of life and relationships.

Proverbs 16:11 *The Lord demands fairness in every business deal; he sets the standard.*

Luke 16:10 *Unless you are faithful in small matters, you won't be faithful in large ones. If you cheat even a little, you won't be honest with greater responsibilities.*

2 Corinthians 4:2 *We reject all shameful and underhanded methods. We do not try to trick anyone, and we do not distort the word of God. We tell the truth before God, and all who are honest know that.*
Integrity is measured in small decisions and choices made when no one else is watching. Wise leaders know that every choice they make will one day come to light.

What is the importance of integrity?
1 Chronicles 29:17 *I know, my God, that you examine our hearts and rejoice when you find integrity there. You know I have done all this with good motives, and I have watched your people offer their gifts willingly and joyously.*
Integrity pleases God.

Proverbs 12:3 *Wickedness never brings stability; only the godly have deep roots.*

Proverbs 10:9 *People with integrity have firm footing, but those who follow crooked paths will slip and fall.*
Integrity provides stability. Each step away from a life of integrity is a step closer to a "slippery slope" that leads into a sinful lifestyle.

Psalm 25:21 *May integrity and honesty protect me, for I put my hope in you.*

Proverbs 11:3 *Good people are guided by their honesty; treacherous people are destroyed by their dishonesty.*
Integrity provides protection and guidance. Sin and the lack of integrity expose you to all kinds of harm, especially the disintegration of your own character.

Psalm 24:3-5 *Who may climb the mountain of the Lord? Who may stand in his holy place? Only those whose hands and hearts are pure, who do not worship idols and never tell lies. They will receive the Lord's blessing and have right standing with God their savior.*

Proverbs 20:7 *The godly walk with integrity; blessed are their children after them.*
Integrity brings God's blessing. Not only does God bless you when you live your life with integrity, but future generations also benefit from your integrity.

Psalm 18:20, 25 *The Lord rewarded me for doing right; he compensated me because of my innocence. . . . To the faithful you show yourself faithful; to those with integrity you show integrity.*
Integrity enables you to continue in uninterrupted fellowship with the Lord and to live under God's care and protection.

How can I develop integrity in my life?
Proverbs 2:1-2, 5, 9 *My child, listen to me and treasure my instructions. Tune your ears to wisdom, and concentrate on understanding. . . . Then you will understand what it means to fear the Lord, and you will gain knowledge of God. . . . Then you will understand what is right, just, and fair, and you will know how to find the right course of action every time.*
Cultivating a right relationship with God and living a life based on God's Word are two essential means to a life of integrity. Look to God and his Word for therein is the standard of integrity.

2 Timothy 2:21 *If you keep yourself pure, you will be a utensil God can use for his purpose. Your life will be clean, and you will be ready for the Master to use you for every good work.*
If you want to be used for godly purposes, commit yourself to a godly life.

How do I demonstrate integrity?

Daniel 6:4 *Then the other administrators and princes began searching for some fault in the way Daniel was handling his affairs, but they couldn't find anything to criticize. He was faithful and honest and always responsible.*

Titus 2:7-8 *And you yourself must be an example to them by doing good deeds of every kind. Let everything you do reflect the integrity and seriousness of your teaching. Let your teaching be so correct that it can't be criticized. Then those who want to argue will be ashamed because they won't have anything bad to say about us.*

You demonstrate integrity by the way you conduct yourself and the way you treat others. Your words and actions are to be consistent and above reproach.

Job 27:4-6 *My lips will speak no evil, and my tongue will speak no lies. I will never concede that you are right; until I die, I will defend my innocence. I will maintain my innocence without wavering. My conscience is clear for as long as I live.*

1 Timothy 1:19 *Cling tightly to your faith in Christ, and always keep your conscience clear. For some people have deliberately violated their consciences; as a result, their faith has been shipwrecked.*

You demonstrate integrity by keeping your conscience clear before God and others.

Deuteronomy 16:19 *You must never twist justice or show partiality. Never accept a bribe, for bribes blind the eyes of the wise and corrupt the decisions of the godly.*

You demonstrate integrity by refusing to twist justice, show partiality, or take bribes.

1 Peter 2:12 *Be careful how you live among your unbelieving neighbors. Even if they accuse you of doing wrong, they will see your honorable behavior, and they will*

believe and give honor to God when he comes to judge the world.

Romans 12:21 *Don't let evil get the best of you, but conquer evil by doing good.*
Living in a non-Christian world with its evils, temptations and sinful pleasures tests a leader's integrity to the limits. You demonstrate your integrity when you guard your every move and seek support and accountability to insure that you maintain integrity in the face of every test.

PROMISE FROM GOD Micah 6:8 *O people, the Lord has already told you what is good, and this is what he requires: to do what is right, to love mercy, and to walk humbly with your God.*

JEALOUSY

See also **COMPETITION, ENVY**

How can jealousy hinder a leader's effectiveness?
1 Samuel 18:6-9 *Women came out from all the towns along the way to celebrate and to cheer for King Saul, and they sang and danced for joy with tambourines and cymbals. This was their song: "Saul has killed his thousands, and David his ten thousands!" This made Saul very angry. "What's this?" he said. "They credit David with ten thousands and me with only thousands. Next they'll be making him their king!" So from that time on Saul kept a jealous eye on David.*
Your leadership can be crippled by jealousy, which may drive your greatest supporters away. (Although the words are often used interchangeably, in this context

we are defining envy primarily as desiring what we don't have, and jealousy as possessiveness and fear of losing what we do have.) Saul was jealous that he would lose the devotion and loyalty of the people because of their admiration for David. You would be wise to celebrate, not compete, with others.

Acts 17:5 *But the Jewish leaders were jealous, so they gathered some worthless fellows from the streets to form a mob.*
Jealousy can make you act in ways diametrically opposed to the values you teach and verbally profess. Jealousy for attention or affection drove the Jewish leaders to manipulation and to extreme action, even seeking to harm or kill others.

Why is jealousy so dangerous?
Proverbs 14:30 *A relaxed attitude lengthens life; jealousy rots it away.*
Jealousy brings decay to your life because it causes you to focus on anger and bitterness.

Proverbs 27:4 *Anger is cruel, . . . but who can survive the destructiveness of jealousy?*
Jealousy tears families and friends apart.

Does jealousy ever have an appropriate place in leadership?
2 Corinthians 11:2 *I am jealous for you with the jealousy of God himself.*

Exodus 20:5 *For I, the Lord your God, am a jealous God who will not share your affection with any other god!*
Jealousy is proper, indeed essential, in the sense of guarding yourself from inappropriate relationships. You need to value your people and your relationship with them by jealously working to protect them.

PROMISE FROM GOD James 3:14-16 *But if you are bitterly jealous and there is selfish ambition in your hearts, don't brag about being wise. That is the worst kind of lie. For jealousy and selfishness are not God's kind of wisdom. Such things are earthly, unspiritual, and motivated by the Devil. For wherever there is jealousy and selfish ambition, there you will find disorder and every kind of evil.*

JESUS CHRIST AS LEADER

What can I learn from Jesus as a leader?

Matthew 5:21-22 *You have heard that the law of Moses says, . . . But I say . . .*

John 8:31-32 *Jesus said to the people who believed in him, "You are truly my disciples if you keep obeying my teachings. And you will know the truth, and the truth will set you free."*
Leaders define reality by developing a worldview and perspective that enables them to interpret life from the eternal vantage point of God's truth. The truth, even when it's hard, sets people free from ignorance and deception. Jesus is truth and sets the standard for truth.

John 5:19 *Jesus replied, "I assure you, the Son can do nothing by himself. He does only what he sees the Father doing. Whatever the Father does, the Son also does."*

John 15:5 *Yes, I am the vine; you are the branches. Those who remain in me, and I in them, will produce much fruit. For apart from me you can do nothing.*
Leaders submit themselves to the ultimate Leader, God.

Mark 3:14 *Then he selected twelve of them to be his regular companions, calling them apostles.*

Mark 6:7 *And he called his twelve disciples together and sent them out two by two.*
Leaders develop teams in community, sharing life and responsibilities, and gaining strength from mutual encouragement and accountability.

Matthew 7:28-29 *After Jesus finished speaking, the crowds were amazed at his teaching, for he taught as one who had real authority—quite unlike the teachers of religious law.*
Leaders teach with insight and practical wisdom.

John 8:46 *Which of you can truthfully accuse me of sin?*
Leaders practice what they preach.

Matthew 10:1 *Jesus called his twelve disciples to him and gave them authority to cast out evil spirits and to heal every kind of disease and illness.*

John 16:13 *When the Spirit of truth comes, he will guide you into all truth.*
Leaders equip and release those they lead. They provide the wisdom and experience necessary, then let go and allow others to take responsibility for the tasks.

Luke 10:17, 20 *When the seventy-two disciples returned, they joyfully reported to him, "Lord, even the demons obey us when we use your name!" . . . "Don't rejoice just because evil spirits obey you; rejoice because your names are registered as citizens of heaven."*
Leaders keep the priorities clear. The disciples were excited to see the power of God at work through them, but Jesus reminded them that the most important fact was the love of God for them.

Mark 10:45 *For even I, the Son of Man, came here not to be served but to serve others, and to give my life as a ransom for many.*

Leaders have a clear sense of mission and dedicate themselves to fulfilling that mission.

Acts 1:8 *But when the Holy Spirit has come upon you, you will receive power and will tell people about me everywhere—in Jerusalem, throughout Judea, in Samaria, and to the ends of the earth.*
Leaders cast a specific vision for those they lead.

John 8:44 *He [the Devil] was a murderer from the beginning and has always hated the truth. There is no truth in him. When he lies, it is consistent with his character; for he is a liar and the father of lies.*
Leaders expose lies and falsehood so that others can think clearly and respond wisely.

Matthew 23:27-28 *How terrible it will be for you teachers of religious law and you Pharisees. Hypocrites! . . . You try to look like upright people outwardly, but inside your hearts are filled with hypocrisy and lawlessness.*
Leaders confront tough situations and people who are harming others.

Luke 9:23, 62 *If any of you wants to be my follower, you must put aside your selfish ambition, shoulder your cross daily, and follow me. . . . Anyone who puts a hand to the plow and then looks back is not fit for the Kingdom of God.*
Leaders expect the most from those they lead and push them to their limits.

Luke 22:29-30 *Just as my Father has granted me a Kingdom, I now grant you the right to eat and drink at my table in that Kingdom. And you will sit on thrones, judging the twelve tribes of Israel.*
Leaders express their love and gratitude

Luke 7:44-46 *Look at this woman kneeling here. When I entered your home, you didn't offer me water to wash the dust from my feet, but she has washed them with her tears and wiped them with her hair. You didn't give me a kiss of greeting, but she has kissed my feet again and again from the time I first came in. You neglected the courtesy of olive oil to anoint my head, but she has anointed my feet with rare perfume.*
Leaders accept expressions of genuine love and gratitude.

Matthew 26:37-38 *He took Peter and Zebedee's two sons, James and John, and he began to be filled with anguish and deep distress. He told them, "My soul is crushed with grief to the point of death. Stay here and watch with me."*
Leaders are vulnerable. Jesus revealed his anguish and expressed his need for the disciples' support as he prayed in Gethsemane, just before his arrest.

John 13:1-5 *Before the Passover celebration, Jesus knew that his hour had come to leave this world and return to his Father. He now showed the disciples the full extent of his love. . . . So he got up from the table, took off his robe, wrapped a towel around his waist, and poured water into a basin. Then he began to wash the disciples' feet and to wipe them with the towel he had around him.*
Leaders serve those they lead in practical, sacrificial, humbling ways.

John 19:18, 30 *There they crucified him. . . . "It is finished!" Then he bowed his head and gave up his spirit.*
Leaders pay the price of love in leadership. None of us will ever compare with Jesus' sacrifice in a literal sense, but all leaders often have to suffer and sacrifice to serve those they lead.

PROMISE FROM GOD John 3:16-17 *For God so loved the world that he gave his only Son, so that everyone who believes in him will not perish but have eternal life. God did not send his Son into the world to condemn it, but to save it.*

JUDGING OTHERS

See **EVALUATION**

JUSTICE

See also **FAIRNESS**

Why is justice essential in leadership?
Isaiah 56:1 *"Be just and fair to all," says the Lord. "Do what is right and good."*

Amos 5:24 *I want to see a mighty flood of justice.*
Leaders must ensure justice, fairness, and equity in their group or organization. There can be no favoritism and no place for multiple standards. Consistency and congruence between values and conduct is vital for your own and your group's credibility.

Proverbs 16:12 *A king despises wrongdoing, for his rule depends on his justice.*

Proverbs 25:4-5 *Remove the dross from silver, and the sterling will be ready for the silversmith. Remove the wicked from the king's court, and his reign will be made secure by justice.*
Wise leaders know that injustice erodes the foundation of a group or organization. Justice, however, will keep you above reproach.

Proverbs 31:8-9 *Speak up for those who cannot speak for themselves; ensure justice for those who are perishing. Yes, speak up for the poor and helpless, and see that they get justice.*
Justice ensures that those who cannot defend themselves are not abused.

1 Kings 3:28 *Word of the king's decision spread quickly throughout all Israel, and the people were awed as they realized the great wisdom God had given him to render decisions with justice.*
A reputation for justice gives people confidence in you as their leader.

How can I cultivate justice?
2 Chronicles 19:6-7 *Always think carefully before pronouncing judgment. Remember that you do not judge to please people but to please the Lord. He will be with you when you render the verdict in each case that comes before you. Fear the Lord and judge with care, for the Lord our God does not tolerate perverted justice, partiality, or the taking of bribes.*
Remember that you ultimately answer to the Lord. Therefore, take time to process your decisions. Understand that not everyone will be pleased with every decision, but you trust that a fair process and integrity will bear fruit in justice and fairness for all.

PROMISE FROM GOD Psalm 58:11 *Then at last everyone will say, "There truly is a reward for those who live for God; surely there is a God who judges justly here on earth."*

LAZINESS

What are the consequences of laziness?

Proverbs 12:24 *Work hard and become a leader; be lazy and become a slave.*
The lazy lose control of their lives and destiny.

Proverbs 18:9 *A lazy person is as bad as someone who destroys things.*
The failure to produce is as bad as wasting what is produced. In both cases, what is needed is not available to those who need it.

Proverbs 21:25 *The desires of lazy people will be their ruin, for their hands refuse to work.*
Desire without action produces frustration and futility. The irony of laziness is that it exaggerates unmet desires while failing to motivate the actions that could fulfill those desires.

Proverbs 20:4 *If you are too lazy to plow in the right season, you will have no food at the harvest.*

Proverbs 24:30-34 *I walked by the field of a lazy person, the vineyard of one lacking sense. I saw that it was overgrown with thorns. It was covered with weeds, and its walls were broken down. Then, as I looked and thought about it, I learned this lesson: A little extra sleep, a little more slumber, a little folding of the hands to rest—and poverty will pounce on you like a bandit; scarcity will attack you like an armed robber.*
Ultimately, laziness brings a person down.

How can I cultivate responsibility instead of laziness in myself and others?

Proverbs 6:6-11 *Take a lesson from the ants, you lazybones. Learn from their ways and be wise! Even though they have no prince, governor, or ruler to make them work, they labor hard all summer, gathering food for the winter. But you, lazybones, how long will you sleep? When will you wake up? I want you to learn this lesson: A little extra sleep, a little more slumber, a little folding of the hands to rest—and poverty will pounce on you like a bandit; scarcity will attack you like an armed robber.*

Observe the progress of others who are successful.

Romans 12:11 *Never be lazy in your work, but serve the Lord enthusiastically.*

Help those you lead to make a commitment to enthusiastic, energetic service.

PROMISE FROM GOD Proverbs 15:19 *A lazy person has trouble all through life; the path of the upright is easy!*

LOVE

See also **RELATIONSHIPS**

How do I express love to those I lead?

John 15:13 *And here is how to measure it—the greatest love is shown when people lay down their lives for their friends.*

Love is willing to sacrifice for the good of others, even to death.

1 Corinthians 13:4-7 *Love is patient and kind. Love is not jealous or boastful or proud or rude. Love does not demand its own way. Love is not irritable, and it keeps no record of when it has been wronged. It is never glad about injustice but rejoices whenever the truth wins out. Love never gives up, never loses faith, is always hopeful, and endures through every circumstance.*

Love is a commitment and a way of acting, not necessarily a feeling. If you practice the qualities and choices described in these verses, you will experience satisfaction and effectiveness beyond imagining.

How do I learn to love the unlovely?

1 John 4:19 *We love each other as a result of his loving us first.*
You find motivation to love in the character, promise, and gift of God, not in the attractiveness or unattractiveness of the other person. Again, love is a decision to value people with respect, compassion, and courtesy because they are created in God's image, not because you feel they are "worthy" of your love.

1 Peter 4:8 *Love covers a multitude of sins.*

1 Corinthians 13:11-13 *When I was a child, I spoke and thought and reasoned as a child does. But when I grew up, I put away childish things. Now we see things imperfectly as in a poor mirror, but then we will see everything with perfect clarity. All that I know now is partial and incomplete, but then I will know everything completely, just as God knows me now. There are three things that will endure—faith, hope, and love—and the greatest of these is love.*
Love is an act of spiritual maturity, based on the eternal significance of each person and of what God is doing in your life. Looking through the dark lenses of this world clouded by sin and suffering, it doesn't always make sense now, for example, to forgive someone who has wounded you deeply or hurt others. But you have God's assurance that when you follow the way of love, you are walking in the way of life.

John 13:34-35 *So I now am giving you a new commandment: Love each other. Just as I have loved you,*

you should love each other. Your love for one another will prove to the world that you are my disciples.
Being a Christian comes with certain expectations, and one of them is that we will love others. Our Christian conduct is proof as to whether we love each other, and loving each other is proof that we belong to Christ.

PROMISE FROM GOD 1 John 4:12 *If we love each other, God lives in us, and his love has been brought to full expression through us.*

LOYALTY

See also **COMMITMENT, FAITHFULNESS, RELATIONSHIPS**

Why is loyalty important?
Proverbs 3:3-4 *Never let loyalty and kindness get away from you! Wear them like a necklace; write them deep within your heart. Then you will find favor with both God and people, and you will gain a good reputation.*

Proverbs 19:22 *Loyalty makes a person attractive. And it is better to be poor than dishonest.*
Leaders understand that loyalty to God and others is essential for the integrity of their relationships and their effectiveness. Without loyalty, others become a means to an end and are not valued for who they are as persons. Your top priority is loyalty to God.

What are the benefits of loyalty?
Ruth 1:16 *I will go wherever you go and live wherever you live. Your people will be my people, and your God will be my God.*
You may find that loyalty is not only a way to value

those God has brought into your life, but it also may open the doors to other benefits. Ruth's loyalty to Naomi not only gave comfort to them both, but it also brought Ruth to faith and into the ancestral line of the promised Messiah.

1 Samuel 19:6-7 *So Saul listened to Jonathan and vowed, "As surely as the Lord lives, David will not be killed." Afterward Jonathan called David and told him what had happened.*
Loyalty not only brings the satisfaction of integrity in a relationship but may also bring practical benefits such as protection and care for your welfare. Jonathan's loyalty to David actually was instrumental in saving David's life on more than one occasion.

Acts 15:37-38 *Barnabas agreed and wanted to take along John Mark. But Paul disagreed strongly, since John Mark had deserted them in Pamphylia and had not shared in their work. Their disagreement over this was so sharp that they separated. Barnabas took John Mark with him and sailed for Cyprus.*
Loyalty can keep the relationship alive so that you can help in restoring one who has failed. Barnabas's persistent loyalty to John Mark made it possible for John Mark to have another opportunity to "prove himself"—and he did (see Colossians 4:10).

PROMISE FROM GOD Psalm 31:23 *For the Lord protects those who are loyal to him.*

MANAGEMENT

See **ORGANIZATION**

MANIPULATION

See **POWER**

MATERIALISM

See **GREED, MONEY**

MENTORING

See also **DELEGATION, PARTNERSHIP, RELATIONSHIPS**

What is mentoring? How does a leader mentor?

Exodus 33:11 *Inside the Tent of Meeting, the Lord would speak to Moses face to face, as a man speaks to his friend. Afterward Moses would return to the camp, but the young man who assisted him, Joshua son of Nun, stayed behind in the Tent of Meeting.*

Joshua 1:1-2 *After the death of Moses the Lord's servant, the Lord spoke to Joshua son of Nun, Moses' assistant. He said, "Now that my servant Moses is dead, you must lead my people across the Jordan River into the land I am giving them."*

Leaders seek to impact the lives of those they lead. You can do this through mentoring. Mentoring is more than formal training; it is sharing life together. Moses and Joshua give an example of effective mentoring. Moses welcomed Joshua into the arena of his own spiritual work, even allowing Joshua to be with him during his most significant experiences with God.

Then, when Moses died, it was clear that Joshua was prepared to assume responsibility as a faithful, fully equipped, credible leader.

2 Timothy 2:2 *You have heard me teach many things that have been confirmed by many reliable witnesses. Teach these great truths to trustworthy people who are able to pass them on to others.*
Leaders have multiple generations in mind. Paul instructs Timothy to think not only about those he is teaching, but also about those they then will teach. From Paul to Timothy, from Timothy to his students, then to his students' students represent four generations! Such long-range vision for changing lives is imperative for leaders who want to make a lasting impact.

Why is mentoring important?
1 Kings 19:16 *Anoint Elisha son of Shaphat from Abel-meholah to replace you as my prophet.*
None of us will live forever in this mortal life, but the work of the Lord continues from generation to generation. Mentoring ensures the continuation of God's work from one generation to the next. The Lord instructed Elijah to prepare his successor Elisha.

PROMISE FROM GOD Romans 15:14 *I am fully convinced, dear brothers and sisters, that you are full of goodness. You know these things so well that you are able to teach others all about them.*

MINISTERS

See **PASTORS/MINISTERS**

MISTAKES

See **FAILURE**

MONEY

See also **DEBT, GREED, PROVISION, STEWARDSHIP**

What do leaders need to understand about money?

Ecclesiastes 5:10 *Those who love money will never have enough. How absurd to think that wealth brings true happiness!*

Wealth alone, regardless of the amount, can never fully satisfy. Money can cultivate a craving—the more you have, the more you want and so on in a vicious cycle that never has a satisfactory conclusion.

1 Timothy 6:6-10 *Yet true religion with contentment is great wealth. After all, we didn't bring anything with us when we came into the world, and we certainly cannot carry anything with us when we die. So if we have enough food and clothing, let us be content. But people who long to be rich fall into temptation and are trapped by many foolish and harmful desires that plunge them into ruin and destruction. For the love of money is at the root of all kinds of evil. And some people, craving money, have wandered from the faith and pierced themselves with many sorrows.*

Leaders are often tempted by money and the possession of, or desire for, worldly goods. Faithfulness often brings success, and success often brings a measure of financial reward. On the one hand, you understand that money is neither good nor bad, but is simply a neutral medium of exchange. On the other hand, money represents wealth, power, and status. As such, it has a tendency to wield extraordinary power over life. Money, like natural resources, material goods, and time itself, is yours to be used for the glory of God, not to take the place of God.

Deuteronomy 8:17-18 *He [the Lord] did it so you would never think that it was your own strength and energy that made you wealthy. Always remember that it is the Lord your God who gives you power to become rich.*
Wealth and prosperity are not your goal as a leader, nor are they definitive signs of God's blessing—for many are poor who are indeed rich in the treasures of heaven. But prosperity, when given by God, is to be received with gratitude and humility, and it is to be shared graciously.

1 Timothy 4:4-5 *Since everything God created is good, we should not reject any of it. We may receive it gladly, with thankful hearts. For we know it is made holy by the word of God and prayer.*
All things are good if received with gratitude and enjoyment in Christ. You will find joy in them especially if you put them to use for ministry, or to share with others.

Hebrews 13:5 *Stay away from the love of money; be satisfied with what you have. For God has said, "I will never fail you. I will never forsake you."*
Your greatest security comes not from what you have, but the fact that God has you.

Isaiah 55:2 *Why spend your money on food that does not give you strength? . . . Listen, and I will tell you where to get food that is good for the soul!*
Too often we buy things to fill a void or a need in our lives. The Bible points to a way to acquire a deep and lasting happiness that always satisfies.

Mark 8:36 *And how do you benefit if you gain the whole world but lose your own soul in the process?*
No amount of money is worth it if it was gained deceptively or dishonestly. Taking advantage of others to make money is stealing. Those who do this lose far more than they could ever gain.

How can I help myself and others deal wisely with money?

Proverbs 28:19 *Hard workers have plenty of food.*

Matthew 25:14 *He called together his servants and gave them money to invest for him while he was gone.*

1 Corinthians 4:12 *We have worked wearily with our own hands to earn our living.*

1 Thessalonians 4:12 *You will not need to depend on others to meet your financial needs.*
Wise leaders teach those they lead God's principles about money, work, and responsibility. You can also model what it means to be a good steward in earning, spending, and saving your money.

1 Timothy 6:17-19 *Tell those who are rich in this world not to be proud and not to trust in their money, which will soon be gone. But their trust should be in the living God, who richly gives us all we need for our enjoyment. Tell them to use their money to do good. They should be rich in good works and should give generously to those in need, always being ready to share with others whatever God has given them. By doing this they will be storing up their treasure as a good foundation for the future so that they may take hold of real life.*
God calls leaders to tell the truth to those they lead. And the truth is that you will be held accountable for how you use the money God has entrusted to you.

Therefore, you should use money in ways that honor God and help others.

Psalm 119:36 *Give me an eagerness for your decrees; do not inflict me with love for money!*
It's wise to pray for a godly attitude toward money and for control over your desires.

Matthew 6:32-33 *Your heavenly Father already knows all your needs, and he will give you all you need from day to day if you live for him and make the Kingdom of God your primary concern.*
Focusing on God's Kingdom can help you overcome the love of money. Remember the character of God, the promises of God, and his faithful provision.

Philippians 4:11-12 *For I have learned how to get along happily whether I have much or little. . . . I have learned the secret of living in every situation.*

Philippians 4:19 *And this same God who takes care of me will supply all your needs from his glorious riches.*
The Bible promises that God will supply all of your needs. The problem comes when your definition of "need" is different from God's. The first thing you must do is study God's Word to discover what he says you need for a fulfilling life.

PROMISE FROM GOD Matthew 6:24 *No one can serve two masters. . . . You cannot serve both God and money.*

MORALITY

See **INTEGRITY**

MOTIVATION

See also **DISCOURAGEMENT, GOALS, TIME, VISION**

Where do I find motivation?

1 Corinthians 9:16 *I am compelled by God to do it. How terrible for me if I didn't do it!*

2 Corinthians 5:14 *Whatever we do, it is because Christ's love controls us.*
Whatever the task, keep the clear sense that you are serving the Lord in all things.

1 Corinthians 3:13-15 *There is going to come a time of testing at the judgment day to see what kind of work each builder has done. Everyone's work will be put through the fire to see whether or not it keeps its value. If the work survives the fire, that builder will receive a reward. But if the work is burned up, the builder will suffer great loss. The builders themselves will be saved, but like someone escaping through a wall of flames.*

2 Corinthians 5:9-10 *So our aim is to please him always, whether we are here in this body or away from this body. For we must all stand before Christ to be judged. We will each receive whatever we deserve for the good or evil we have done in our bodies.*
The reality of one day standing before Jesus and having to account for all you have done should motivate you to avoid what is wrong or worthless. For a follower of Christ, there is no judgment of salvation (for he has already forgiven you), but there is a judgment of evaluation, when your good works will be assessed. You will be rewarded according to your faithfulness—or lack thereof.

How do I stay motivated when I am discouraged?

2 Corinthians 4:1 *Since God in his mercy has given us this wonderful ministry, we never give up.*
Let your sense of God's presence, God's call, and God's love as seen in his mercy sustain you even when outward circumstances threaten to discourage or even crush you.

Matthew 6:33 *He will give you all you need from day to day if you live for him and make the Kingdom of God your primary concern.*
A clear, ever-growing vision for the Kingdom of God and joyful trust in God's promises will sustain your motivation.

Jeremiah 20:9 *If I say I'll never mention the Lord or speak in his name, his word burns in my heart like a fire. It's like a fire in my bones! I am weary of holding it in!*
That which God gives you becomes like a burning passion within. Even when you try to resist it or escape, you cannot.

Matthew 23:37 *O Jerusalem, Jerusalem, . . . how often I have wanted to gather your children together as a hen protects her chicks beneath her wings, but you wouldn't let me.*

Matthew 25:40 *I assure you, when you did it to one of the least of these my brothers and sisters, you were doing it to me!*
Motivation can also be renewed by realizing afresh your call to compassion for others.

PROMISE FROM GOD Colossians 3:17 *And whatever you do or say, let it be as a representative of the Lord Jesus, all the while giving thanks through him to God the Father.*

NEGOTIATION

How do I negotiate effectively and appropriately?

Genesis 18:23-32 *Abraham . . . said, ". . . Suppose you find fifty innocent people there within the city—will you still destroy it, and not spare it for their sakes? Surely you wouldn't do such a thing, destroying the innocent with the guilty." . . . And the Lord replied, "If I find fifty innocent people in Sodom, I will spare the entire city for their sake." . . . Finally, Abraham said, "Lord, please do not get angry; I will speak but once more! Suppose only ten are found there?" And the Lord said, "Then, for the sake of the ten, I will not destroy it."*

Explore the possibilities of achieving a win-win with others through negotiation. Negotiation is a process that involves respect and understanding of what both parties are seeking. In this passage, Abraham "negotiates" with the Lord concerning the threatened judgment on Sodom. This passage should not be read as antagonistic bickering to get a better deal with God, but as a humble exploration of God's mercy.

What are the benefits of negotiation?

1 Samuel 25:32-33 *David replied to Abigail, "Praise the Lord, the God of Israel, who has sent you to meet me today! Thank God for your good sense! Bless you for keeping me from murdering the man and carrying out vengeance with my own hands."*

We would do well to study the entire story of Abigail's negotiation to prevent David from taking revenge for the insults by her husband, Nabal. She got David's attention by addressing his immediate need for food and then showed respect by honoring him. She then called him to consider his own conscience and how he would look back on this experience if he acted rashly.

Because he listened and considered these things, David spared himself and many others a great deal of grief.

Acts 9:26-28 *When Saul arrived in Jerusalem, he tried to meet with the believers, but they were all afraid of him. They thought he was only pretending to be a believer! Then Barnabas brought him to the apostles and told them how Saul had seen the Lord on the way to Damascus. Barnabas also told them what the Lord had said to Saul and how he boldly preached in the name of Jesus in Damascus. Then the apostles accepted Saul.*
Barnabas's negotiation with the believers in Jerusalem not only secured Saul's acceptance, but it paved the way for the ministry of one of the most influential Christian leaders of all time.

Acts 15:1-2 *While Paul and Barnabas were at Antioch of Syria, some men from Judea arrived and began to teach the Christians: "Unless you keep the ancient Jewish custom of circumcision taught by Moses, you cannot be saved." Paul and Barnabas, disagreeing with them, argued forcefully and at length. Finally, Paul and Barnabas were sent to Jerusalem, accompanied by some local believers, to talk to the apostles and elders about this question.*
Leaders utilize negotiation to preserve community while at the same time maintaining the integrity of their values. In this case, the intentional deliberation and negotiation of the early church leaders preserved the integrity of the gospel message of grace while at the same time calling the people to conduct their lives in ways that encouraged mutual respect.

PROMISE FROM GOD Matthew 5:9 *God blesses those who work for peace, for they will be called the children of God.*

OFFICERS OF THE CHURCH

See **DEACONS, ELDERS, PASTORS/MINISTERS**

ORGANIZATION

What do organization and administration do for me as a leader and those I lead?

Genesis 2:15 *The Lord God placed the man in the Garden of Eden to tend and care for it.*
God charged human beings with the continuing work of bringing order out of chaos so that the earth would be fruitful. Organization is the holy task of ordering and administrating human and material resources and time in ways that bring out the best in people and situations.

Genesis 6:19 *Bring a pair of every kind of animal—a male and a female—into the boat with you to keep them alive during the flood.*

Genesis 41:39-40 *Turning to Joseph, Pharaoh said, "Since God has revealed the meaning of the dreams to you, you are the wisest man in the land! I hereby appoint you to direct this project. You will manage my household and organize all my people. Only I will have a rank higher than yours."*
Some believe that organization is human manipulation that drives (or at least omits) the Holy Spirit from a situation. The testimony throughout Scripture, however, shows that God works in orderly ways. In fact, organization not only improves the quality of life, but can also literally save lives. Noah's organizational skills, in obedience to God's commands, preserved his life, his family's lives, and the animal species during

the Flood. Joseph was used by God to organize the Egyptian nation so that the future years of bumper crops could be stored and then distributed during the seven years of famine.

How do I organize myself and others?

Numbers 1:20-21 *This is the number of men twenty years old or older who were able to go to war, each listed according to his own clan and family.*

Numbers 2:1-2 *Then the Lord gave these instructions to Moses and Aaron: "Each tribe will be assigned its own area in the camp, and the various groups will camp beneath their family banners. The Tabernacle will be located at the center of these tribal compounds."*
Leaders know that accomplishment through community requires organization in order to prevent chaos and mishap. In preparation for their journey through the wilderness, the opening chapters of Numbers tell how Moses, under God's direction, organized the people in a variety of ways for communication, for coordination in travel, for protection, and for regulation of their spiritual nurture.

1 Corinthians 12:27-28 *Now all of you together are Christ's body, and each one of you is a separate and necessary part of it. Here is a list of some of the members that God has placed in the body of Christ.*

1 Corinthians 14:26 *When you meet, one will sing, another will teach, another will tell some special revelation God has given, one will speak in an unknown language, while another will interpret what is said. But everything that is done must be useful to all and build them up in the Lord.*
Leaders help each person to understand his or her role in the group. Taking time to organize and train each

person values all the people involved and helps them utilize their gifts and abilities to the fullest.

PROMISE FROM GOD 1 Corinthians 14:33 *For God is not a God of disorder but of peace.*

PARTNERSHIP

See also **ACCOUNTABILITY, MENTORING, RELATIONSHIPS**

Why do leaders need to consider having partners?
Ecclesiastes 4:9-10 *Two people can accomplish more than twice as much as one; they get a better return for their labor. If one person falls, the other can reach out and help. But people who are alone when they fall are in real trouble.*
Leaders are tempted to be "lone rangers." Sometimes they feel this is necessary, but other times it's because they don't want to be bothered with the complexities and demands of involving others. But the lone leader is vulnerable in many ways. Wise leaders find partners who will provide mutual support, wisdom, accountability, and companionship.

What are some cautions about partnership?
Proverbs 22:26-27 *Do not co-sign another person's note or put up a guarantee for someone else's loan. If you can't pay it, even your bed will be snatched from under you.*
Irresponsible partners can put leaders in jeopardy.

2 Chronicles 16:7 *At that time Hanani the seer came to King Asa and told him, "Because you have put your*

trust in the king of Aram instead of in the Lord your God, you missed your chance to destroy the army of the king of Aram."

2 Chronicles 18:1 *Now Jehoshaphat enjoyed great riches and high esteem, and he arranged for his son to marry the daughter of King Ahab of Israel.*

2 Chronicles 20:35 *But near the end of his life, King Jehoshaphat of Judah made an alliance with King Ahaziah of Israel, who was a very wicked man.*
Partners should never replace reliance on the Lord, nor compromise obedience to God. In each of these situations, the kings chose to rely on human alliances for military or business purposes instead of trusting and honoring God's words and call.

2 Corinthians 6:14-15 *Don't team up with those who are unbelievers. How can goodness be a partner with wickedness? How can light live with darkness? What harmony can there be between Christ and the Devil? How can a believer be a partner with an unbeliever?*
Partnership, in business or marriage, is teaming up with another to act as one. God warns against partnerships in which one loves God and the other doesn't because these will naturally lead to conflict or to spiritual compromise.

PROMISE FROM GOD Ecclesiastes 4:12 *A person standing alone can be attacked and defeated, but two can stand back-to-back and conquer. Three are even better, for a triple-braided cord is not easily broken.*

PASTORS/MINISTERS

How are pastors to lead?

Ephesians 4:9-13 *Christ first came down to the lowly world in which we live. . . . He is the one who gave these gifts to the church: the apostles, the prophets, the evangelists, and the pastors and teachers. Their responsibility is to equip God's people to do his work and build up the church, the body of Christ, until we come to such unity in our faith and knowledge of God's Son that we will be mature and full grown in the Lord, measuring up to the full stature of Christ.*

God has provided pastors to provide unique spiritual instruction, leadership, and care for his people. Pastors are not better people, nor are they somehow different than other Christians. But they have been called to the service of spiritual leadership so that all God's people will mature and serve in the building of God's Kingdom. It's essential to realize that the ministry belongs to all the people. Pastors are like coaches who help the people do their best on God's team.

Exodus 28:29 *In this way, Aaron will carry the names of the tribes of Israel on the chestpiece over his heart when he goes into the presence of the Lord in the Holy Place.*

Compassion and spiritual direction are at the heart of spiritual leadership. The high priest wore the names of the tribes of Israel on his chest as a symbol of carrying people in his heart in prayer and godly concern.

Ezekiel 3:17-18 *Son of man, I have appointed you as a watchman for Israel. Whenever you receive a message from me, pass it on to the people immediately. If I warn the wicked, . . . but you fail to deliver the warning, . . . I will hold you responsible.*

Church leaders are watchmen or guardians of the community of faith who communicate God's word of nurture, instruction, and warning to God's people. They cannot force the people to listen, but they must convey God's Word clearly, boldly calling them to obedience. Otherwise, the people will continue in disobedience, not knowing God's will, and the pastors will be held responsible for the people's sins.

Ezekiel 34:11-16 *For this is what the Sovereign Lord says: I myself will search and find my sheep. I will be like a shepherd looking for his scattered flock. I will find my sheep and rescue them from all the places to which they were scattered on that dark and cloudy day. I will bring them back home. . . . I will search for my lost ones who strayed away, and I will bring them safely home again. I will bind up the injured and strengthen the weak.*

1 Peter 5:1-2 *And now, a word to you who are elders in the churches. . . . Care for the flock of God entrusted to you. Watch over it willingly, not grudgingly—not for what you will get out of it, but because you are eager to serve God.*

The Lord models what it means to be a good shepherd (pastor) of his people. The first priority is bringing people "into the fold," both through conversion of unbelievers, as well as seeking out and restoring those who have become alienated from God's people. Then they care for them through worship, instruction, spiritual refreshment, and nourishment. Then they call the people of God to live together in godly fellowship.

PROMISE FROM GOD James 3:1 *Dear brothers and sisters, not many of you should become teachers in the church, for we who teach will be judged by God with greater strictness.*

PEER PRESSURE

See **COMPETITION**

PERSEVERANCE

See also **SETBACKS, TRIALS/TROUBLE**

Who are some leaders who persevered in the Bible?

Genesis 17:1-2, 19 *When Abram was ninety-nine years old, the Lord appeared to him and said, "I am God Almighty; serve me faithfully and live a blameless life. I will make a covenant with you, by which I will guarantee to make you into a mighty nation. . . . Sarah, your wife, will bear you a son. You will name him Isaac, and I will confirm my everlasting covenant with him and his descendants."*
Abram persevered in trusting the promises of God.

2 Samuel 5:4 *David was thirty years old when he began to reign, and he reigned forty years in all.*
David persevered in waiting on the timing of God. Many scholars believe David waited at least thirteen to seventeen years for God's promise that he would be anointed king to come true. Most of this time he actually spent running from Saul who was determined to kill him.

2 Corinthians 11:23-29 *I have worked harder, been put in jail more often, been whipped times without number, and faced death again and again. . . . I have lived with weariness and pain and sleepless nights. Often I have been hungry and thirsty and have gone without food. Often I have shivered with cold, without enough clothing to keep me warm. Then, besides all this, I have the daily burden of*

how the churches are getting along. Who is weak without my feeling that weakness? Who is led astray, and I do not burn with anger?
Paul persevered through innumerable trials in God's service.

Why is perseverance so important?
2 Corinthians 8:10-11 *I suggest that you finish what you started a year ago, for you were the first to propose this idea, and . . . the first to begin doing something about it. Now you should carry this project through to completion just as enthusiastically as you began it.*
Perseverance validates your promises and demonstrates your credibility.

Matthew 7:7 *Keep on asking, and you will be given what you ask for. Keep on looking, and you will find. Keep on knocking, and the door will be opened.*
God honors persistence in prayer.

Romans 5:3-4 *We can rejoice, too, when we run into problems and trials, for we know that they are good for us—they help us learn to endure. And endurance develops strength of character in us, and character strengthens our confident expectation of salvation.*

James 1:2-4 *Dear brothers and sisters, whenever trouble comes your way, let it be an opportunity for joy. For when your faith is tested, your endurance has a chance to grow. So let it grow, for when your endurance is fully developed, you will be strong in character and ready for anything.*
Perseverance produces godliness, love, productivity, usefulness, growth, strength of character, preparedness, strong faith, and eternal rewards.

1 Peter 2:19 *For God is pleased with you when, for the sake of your conscience, you patiently endure unfair treatment.*
Endurance honors God and his plan for you.

1 Peter 4:13 *Instead, be very glad—because these trials will make you partners with Christ in his suffering, and afterward you will have the wonderful joy of sharing his glory when it is displayed to all the world.*

James 1:12 *God blesses the people who patiently endure testing. Afterward they will receive the crown of life that God has promised to those who love him.*
If you persevere in your faith, you will share in the eternal riches of Christ.

2 Corinthians 1:6 *So when we are weighed down with troubles, it is for your benefit and salvation! For when God comforts us, it is so that we, in turn, can be an encouragement to you. Then you can patiently endure the same things we suffer.*
Your perseverance encourages others.

How do I develop endurance and the stamina to persevere?

Philippians 1:6 *And I am sure that God, who began the good work within you, will continue his work until it is finally finished on that day when Christ Jesus comes back again.*
Your perseverance is based on the promise of God's persistent, faithful work in your life. God never stops working in you.

Habakkuk 2:3 *But these things I plan won't happen right away. Slowly, steadily, surely, the time approaches when the vision will be fulfilled. If it seems slow, wait patiently, for it will surely take place. It will not be delayed.*

Develop realistic expectations in order to persevere.

2 Corinthians 4:1 *And so, since God in his mercy has given us this wonderful ministry, we never give up.*
Find strength in your call and confidence that, no matter how things appear outwardly, God has given you your work to do.

2 Thessalonians 3:5 *May the Lord bring you into an ever deeper understanding of the love of God and the endurance that comes from Christ.*

Habakkuk 3:19 *The Sovereign Lord is my strength! He will make me as surefooted as a deer and bring me safely over the mountains.*
Endurance originates with God. He is your source of the power and perseverance you need to endure.

Hebrews 12:1-3 *Therefore, since we are surrounded by such a huge crowd of witnesses to the life of faith, let us strip off every weight that slows us down, especially the sin that so easily hinders our progress. And let us run with endurance the race that God has set before us. We do this by keeping our eyes on Jesus, on whom our faith depends from start to finish. . . . Think about all he endured when sinful people did such terrible things to him, so that you don't become weary and give up.*
The faithfulness of God's people across the ages and, above all, the example of Jesus give you models of perseverance on which to focus and model your own faithfulness.

1 Thessalonians 1:3 *As we talk to our God and Father about you, we think of your faithful work, your loving deeds, and your continual anticipation of the return of our Lord Jesus Christ.*
Develop endurance by maintaining an eternal perspective inspired by hope.

PROMISE FROM GOD Matthew 24:13 *But those who endure to the end will be saved.*

PERSISTENCE

See **PERSEVERANCE**

PERSONAL DISCIPLINE

See also **SPIRITUAL DISCIPLINES, TIME**

Why is personal discipline necessary for leaders?

Proverbs 23:23 *Get the truth and don't ever sell it; also get wisdom, discipline, and discernment.*
Leaders know that personal discipline, not innate talent or intellect, is often the deciding factor between success and failure.

1 Kings 10:23—11:4 *So King Solomon became richer and wiser than any other king in all the earth. . . . Now King Solomon loved many foreign women. . . . In Solomon's old age, they turned his heart to worship their gods instead of trusting only in the Lord his God, as his father, David, had done.*
A leader's discipline, or lack thereof, greatly affects others' welfare.

How do I cultivate personal discipline?

Philippians 3:12-15 *But I keep working toward that day when I will finally be all that Christ Jesus saved me for and wants me to be. No, dear brothers and sisters, I am still not all I should be, but I am focusing all my energies on this one thing: Forgetting the past and looking forward to what lies ahead, I strain to reach the end of the race and receive the prize for which God, through Christ Jesus, is calling us up to heaven. I hope all of you who are mature Christians will agree on these things.*

Discipline begins with passion and is sustained by power. For Jesus' followers, the passion is your clear sense of God's call for your life to glorify him in all things. And the power comes for the Holy Spirit at work within you (see Philippians 2:12-13).

1 Corinthians 9:24-26 *Remember that in a race everyone runs, but only one person gets the prize. You also must run in such a way that you will win. All athletes practice strict self-control. They do it to win a prize that will fade away, but we do it for an eternal prize. So I run straight to the goal with purpose in every step.*

Discipline is the link between your desires and achieving those desires. Self-control not only helps you achieve your goals, but also helps you maintain them. Many leaders have been ruined by letting up on discipline once they have achieved their goals.

1 Timothy 4:7-8 *Spend your time and energy in training yourself for spiritual fitness. Physical exercise has some value, but spiritual exercise is much more important, for it promises a reward in both this life and the next.*

Discipline requires time, effort, hard work, and even suffering. But these are like the efforts of a farmer who knows they will produce a harvest, or of musicians who know that their freedom to make music comes from their effort in practice.

PROMISE FROM GOD Proverbs 1:7 *Fear of the Lord is the beginning of knowledge. Only fools despise wisdom and discipline.*

PLANNING

See **ORGANIZATION**

POWER

See also **AUTHORITY, SERVANTHOOD**

Why must a leader understand the nature of power?
Deuteronomy 8:17-18 *He [the Lord] did it so you would never think that it was your own strength and energy that made you wealthy. Always remember that it is the Lord your God who gives you power to become rich.* Leaders have the ability to influence others, to mobilize resources, and to get the attention of significant people or groups of people in society. They can make things happen—or keep things from happening. In short, they have power to control. This is the most seductive aspect of leadership—but is also at the heart of effectiveness. Ultimately, however, leaders in all walks of life are dependent on God's power. There are no "self-made" people who have power in and of themselves. You cannot claim responsibility for your birth, your genetic makeup, nor the political, economic, and social circumstances and times into which you were born. God allows you to live at the time and place of his choosing. Remember where your power comes from so that you will use it in accordance with God's values and will.

What happens when leaders abuse their power?
1 Kings 12:16 *When all Israel realized that the king had rejected their request, they shouted, "Down with David and his dynasty! We have no share in Jesse's son! Let's go*

home, Israel! Look out for your own house, O David!" So the people of Israel returned home.
Abusing power leads to abusing people, which leads to conflict and even open rebellion. Rehoboam, Solomon's son, desired to show power and rejected the advice of older wise men. The result was a civil war from which Israel never recovered.

PROMISE FROM GOD Ephesians 3:20 *Now glory be to God! By his mighty power at work within us, he is able to accomplish infinitely more than we would ever dare to ask or hope.*

PRAYER

See also **SPIRITUAL DISCIPLINES**

What role does prayer play in my life as a leader?
1 Samuel 12:23 *As for me, I will certainly not sin against the Lord by ending my prayers for you.*
Consistently pray for those you lead.

Exodus 32:11 *But Moses pleaded with the Lord his God. . . . "O Lord!" he exclaimed. "Why are you so angry with your own people whom you brought from the land of Egypt with such great power and mighty acts?"*
Pray for the Lord's mercy on the people. This does not mean that you don't confront the people's sin, however. Moses' intercession saved the disobedient Israelites from the punishment of God's wrath.

1 Kings 8:22-23 *Then Solomon stood with his hands lifted toward heaven before the altar of the Lord in front of the entire community of Israel. He prayed . . .*
Pray publicly at times, reminding your people that they can depend on the promises and power of God.

2 Chronicles 20:3-6 *Jehoshaphat was alarmed by this news and sought the Lord for guidance. He also gave orders that everyone throughout Judah should observe a fast. So people from all the towns of Judah came to Jerusalem to seek the Lord. Jehoshaphat stood before the people of Judah and Jerusalem in front of the new courtyard at the Temple of the Lord. He prayed . . .*
Pray when you don't know exactly what to do, or when you don't have the resources you need for a crisis or situation.

Luke 22:31-32 *Simon, Simon, Satan has asked to have all of you, to sift you like wheat. But I have pleaded in prayer for you, Simon, that your faith should not fail. So when you have repented and turned to me again, strengthen and build up your brothers.*
Pray for the spiritual protection of those you lead.

Colossians 1:9 *So we have continued praying for you ever since we first heard about you. We ask God to give you a complete understanding of what he wants to do in your lives, and we ask him to make you wise with spiritual wisdom.*
Pray for the spiritual growth and maturity of those you lead.

PROMISE FROM GOD James 5:16 *The earnest prayer of a righteous person has great power and wonderful results.*

PREPARATION

See **ORGANIZATION**

PRESSURE

See **STRESS**

PRIDE

See also **AMBITION, FLATTERY, HUMILITY**

Why must leaders beware of pride?

Psalm 18:27 *You rescue those who are humble, but you humiliate the proud.*

Proverbs 16:18 *Pride goes before destruction, and haughtiness before a fall.*
God delivers the humble but humiliates the proud.

2 Chronicles 26:16 *But when he had become powerful, he also became proud, which led to his downfall.*
An inflated estimation of your past successes leads to prideful behavior and, ultimately, judgment. King Uzziah (also known as Azariah) pridefully thought his position and success made him immune from the standards to which all others were subject. God judged him for his presumption.

Obadiah 3 *You are proud because you live in a rock fortress and make your home high in the mountains.*
Pride finds comfort in false security.

Acts 12:22-23 *The people gave him a great ovation, shouting, "It is the voice of a god, not of a man!" Instantly, an angel of the Lord struck Herod with a sickness, because he accepted the people's worship instead of giving the glory to God.*
God hates pride and will judge it severely.

1 Corinthians 10:12-13 *If you think you are standing strong, be careful, for you, too, may fall into the same sin. But remember that the temptations that come into your life are no different from what others experience.*
Pride can blind you to your vulnerability to temptation and lead you to repeat the sins of the past.

When is pride healthy and appropriate?
Romans 15:17 *So it is right for me to be enthusiastic about all Christ Jesus has done through me.*
You can feel satisfaction in what God does through you. Paul was proud not of what he had accomplished but of what God had done through him.

2 Corinthians 5:12-13 *Are we trying to pat ourselves on the back again? No, . . . it is to bring glory to God.*
Like Paul, you can feel a holy pride in the integrity and honesty of your ministry and life.

Galatians 6:14 *God forbid that I should boast about anything except the cross of our Lord Jesus Christ.*
You should be most proud of what Christ has done in saving his people from sin and death.

PROMISE FROM GOD Matthew 23:12 *But those who exalt themselves will be humbled, and those who humble themselves will be exalted.*

PRIORITIES

See **GOALS, ORGANIZATION**

PROBLEMS

See **CONFLICT, TRIALS/TROUBLE**

PROCRASTINATION

See **LAZINESS**

PROMISES

See also **INTEGRITY**

Why is it important for leaders to keep their promises?

Numbers 30:2 *A man who makes a vow to the Lord or makes a pledge under oath must never break it.* Whether in a relationship with the Lord or with people, leaders know that people rely on their promises. Keeping a promise is the basic foundation for trust in any relationship.

2 Samuel 9:7 *But David said, "Don't be afraid! I've asked you to come so that I can be kind to you because of my vow to your father, Jonathan."* Leaders honor God and others by keeping their promises. David had promised Jonathan to care for his family, and he kept his word when he became king. David took Jonathan's crippled son (Saul's grandson, Mephibosheth) into his household to care for him.

What should I keep in mind as I consider making a promise?

Ecclesiastes 5:2-5 *And don't make rash promises to God, for he is in heaven, and you are only here on earth.*

So let your words be few. . . . So when you make a promise to God, don't delay in following through, for God takes no pleasure in fools. Keep all the promises you make to him. It is better to say nothing than to promise something that you don't follow through on.
Do not make promises quickly, and do not take them lightly.

PROMISE FROM GOD Hebrews 10:23 *God can be trusted to keep his promise.*

PROSPERITY

See **MONEY**

PROVISION

See also **MONEY**

Where do leaders turn when they need provision?
Philippians 4:6 *Don't worry about anything; instead, pray about everything. Tell God what you need, and thank him for all he has done.*
Leaders trust that where God guides, God provides. Release your anxieties to the Lord whose love is certain and whose abilities are more than adequate to supply all you truly need.

Matthew 6:31-33 *So don't worry about having enough food or drink or clothing. Why be like the pagans who are so deeply concerned about these things? Your heavenly Father already knows all your needs, and he will give you all you need from day to day if you live for him and make the Kingdom of God your primary concern.*

Leaders keep their focus on their priorities, trusting that the necessary provisions will be supplied.

Exodus 16:4 *Then the Lord said to Moses, "Look, I'm going to rain down food from heaven for you."*
We most often experience God's provision when we are following him in obedience. God provided for the daily needs of his people in marvelous ways—and continues to do so.

2 Peter 1:3 *As we know Jesus better, his divine power gives us everything we need for living a godly life.*
God has provided resources from his own character to those who seek him.

2 Corinthians 9:8 *And God will generously provide all you need. Then you will always have everything you need and plenty left over to share with others.*
God's provision to us is also meant to become his provision through us, to continue his work in the world.

PROMISES FROM GOD Psalm 23:1-3 *The Lord is my shepherd; I have everything I need. He lets me rest in green meadows; he leads me beside peaceful streams. He renews my strength. He guides me along right paths, bringing honor to his name.*

Philippians 4:19 *And this same God who takes care of me will supply all your needs from his glorious riches, which have been given to us in Christ Jesus.*

PURPOSE/MISSION

See **GOALS, MOTIVATION, VISION**

QUITTING

See **PERSEVERANCE**

RECONCILIATION

See **FORGIVENESS**

RELATIONSHIPS

See also **LOVE, LOYALTY, MENTORING, PARTNERSHIP**

Why are relationships important to leaders?
Genesis 2:18 *And the Lord God said, "It is not good for the man to be alone. I will make a companion who will help him."*
People were created as relational beings, and leaders are no exception. Leadership is not simply about getting things done, but getting things done through, with, and for people. Relationships, therefore, are a central element of leadership. In many ways, people are the product of all we do.

Why does it often feel "lonely at the top"?
Numbers 11:14 *I can't carry all these people by myself! The load is far too heavy!*
It can be lonely at the top, partially because only the leader understands the full burden of the organization, the cares of the people, and the demands of the "big picture." You feel ultimately responsible for the care of your people and the success of the project. You may also be lonely because you wonder whom you can

trust. You need to develop relationships with people with whom you are "safe" and with whom you can be candid.

How can I build healthy relationships with others?

John 15:12 *I command you to love each other in the same way that I love you.*

Proverbs 17:17 *A friend is always loyal, and a brother is born to help in time of need.*

Ephesians 4:32 *Instead, be kind to each other, tenderhearted, forgiving one another, just as God through Christ has forgiven you.*

1 Peter 2:17 *Show respect for everyone. Love your Christian brothers and sisters. Fear God. Show respect for the king.*

Colossians 3:13 *You must make allowance for each other's faults and forgive the person who offends you. Remember, the Lord forgave you, so you must forgive others.*

The foundation of healthy relationships is love, and the four cornerstones are loyalty, kindness, respect, and forgiveness.

PROMISE FROM GOD Ecclesiastes 4:9-10 *Two people can accomplish more than twice as much as one; they get a better return for their labor. If one person falls, the other can reach out and help. But people who are alone when they fall are in real trouble.*

REPUTATION

See also CHARACTER

Why should leaders care about reputation?

Proverbs 22:1 *Choose a good reputation over great riches, for being held in high esteem is better than having silver or gold.*

Take care to build a reputation of integrity so the credibility of your witness is not questioned and the ministry of the gospel is not hindered.

How can I cultivate a good reputation?

Matthew 6:1 *Don't do your good deeds publicly, to be admired.*

Jesus warns not to pursue spirituality in order to impress others.

Proverbs 3:1-4 *My child, never forget the things I have taught you. Store my commands in your heart, for they will give you a long and satisfying life. Never let loyalty and kindness get away from you! Wear them like a necklace; write them deep within your heart. Then you will find favor with both God and people, and you will gain a good reputation.*

Following God's direction in Scripture and treating people with respect are two essential ingredients in developing a godly reputation.

PROMISE FROM GOD 1 Peter 5:6 *Humble yourselves under the mighty power of God, and in his good time he will honor you.*

RESPONSIBILITY

See also STEWARDSHIP

Why is the willingness to carry responsibility important for leadership?

Isaiah 6:8 *Then I heard the Lord asking, "Whom should I send as a messenger to my people? Who will go for us?" And I said, "Lord, I'll go! Send me."*
Responsibility is the heart of leadership, for the leader is the one who responds to a need. That response may be to God's call or to the needs you see around you.

Ezekiel 22:30 *I looked for someone who might rebuild the wall of righteousness that guards the land. I searched for someone to stand in the gap in the wall so I wouldn't have to destroy the land, but I found no one.*
If no one takes responsibility for the spiritual welfare of the group, they can fall into disobedience and suffer dreadful consequences. Wise leadership can protect the group from such problems.

How do I develop responsibility?

Galatians 6:5 *For we are each responsible for our own conduct.*
You develop responsibility by using the gifts God has entrusted to you.

Romans 12:3 *As God's messenger, I give each of you this warning: Be honest in your estimate of yourselves, measuring your value by how much faith God has given you.*
You can become more responsible by assessing how much responsibility you can handle, and then making sure that you handle it well.

PROMISE FROM GOD Matthew 25:29 *To those who use well what they are given, even more will be given, and they will have an abundance. But from those who are unfaithful, even what little they have will be taken away.*

RESOURCES

See **PROVISION**

REST

See **BALANCE, BURNOUT, SABBATH**

RETIREMENT

What does the Bible say about retirement?

Joshua 14:10-11 *Now, as you can see, the Lord has kept me alive and well as he promised for all these forty-five years since Moses made this promise—even while Israel wandered in the wilderness. Today I am eighty-five years old. I am as strong now as I was when Moses sent me on that journey, and I can still travel and fight as well as I could then.*

The Bible does not give an age for retirement, with the exception of the Levites who served in the demanding work of the Tabernacle. The ages of retirement are established by business, based on economical concerns or physical limitations, but need not dictate your attitude toward work that falls outside the scope of mandatory retirement.

What should I consider as the time approaches for me to release a particular aspect of my responsibilities?

Joshua 13:1 *When Joshua was an old man, the Lord said to him, "You are growing old, and much land remains to be conquered."*

Numbers 20:26 *There you will remove Aaron's priestly garments and put them on Eleazar, his son. Aaron will die there and join his ancestors.*

Work must continue after you. Since there is typically a need for a successor, it is good to plan for succession before the day comes when the successor is needed.

How can I best prepare for retirement from a particular job or career?

Proverbs 16:31 *Gray hair is a crown of glory; it is gained by living a godly life.*

Proverbs 17:6 *Grandchildren are the crowning glory of the aged; parents are the pride of their children.*

The most important aspects of life continue on through retirement—relationships. Your relationship with God should continue to grow as you live a godly life, fully trusting in him. Retirement affords you the opportunity to give even more focus to your relationships, with the Lord and with your extended family.

How can I continue to be productive in my retirement years?

Hebrews 6:11 *Our great desire is that you will keep right on loving others as long as life lasts.*

By continuing to love others.

2 Peter 1:8 *The more you grow like this, the more you will become productive and useful in your knowledge of our Lord Jesus Christ.*

By continuing to grow and learn spiritually.

Psalm 92:12 *But the godly will flourish like palm trees and grow strong like the cedars of Lebanon.*
By living a godly life and teaching others to do the same.

1 Corinthians 12:5 *There are different kinds of service in the church, but it is the same Lord we are serving.*
By being flexible to changes in your roles as you continue to serve the Lord.

Titus 3:14 *For our people should not have unproductive lives. They must learn to do good by helping others who have urgent needs.*
By helping others with all the strength and energy God supplies.

Proverbs 20:29 *The glory of the young is their strength; the gray hair of experience is the splendor of the old.*

Job 12:12-13 *Wisdom belongs to the aged, and understanding to those who have lived many years. But true wisdom and power are with God; counsel and understanding are his.*
By valuing your experience, wisdom, and understanding as gifts from God. Continue to worship, praise, hope, rejoice, trust, grow, search, obey, do right, serve, and faithfully endure to the end.

PROMISE FROM GOD Isaiah 46:4 *I will be your God throughout your lifetime—until your hair is white with age. I made you, and I will care for you. I will carry you along and save you.*

REWARDS

What rewards do leaders experience?

Philippians 4:1 *Dear brothers and sisters, I love you and long to see you, for you are my joy and the reward for my work. So please stay true to the Lord, my dear friends.*
Leaders' greatest rewards are seeing their positive impact in changed lives.

Numbers 14:24 *My servant Caleb is different from the others. He has remained loyal to me, and I will bring him into the land he explored. His descendants will receive their full share of that land.*
Faithfulness to God will be rewarded with blessings for you and for your descendants.

2 Samuel 22:25-27 *The Lord rewarded me for doing right, because of my innocence in his sight. To the faithful you show yourself faithful; to those with integrity you show integrity. To the pure you show yourself pure, but to the wicked you show yourself hostile.*
Faithful leaders know God more deeply and experience the grace of God's faithfulness.

Luke 19:17 *You have been faithful with the little I have entrusted to you, so you will be governor of ten cities as your reward.*
God rewards leaders who have been faithful in small things with greater opportunities.

Hebrews 3:14 *If we are faithful to the end, . . . we will share in all that belongs to Christ.*
Heavenly rewards await those who are faithful to God.

PROMISE FROM GOD Revelation 2:10
Remain faithful even when facing death, and I will give you the crown of life.

RISK

What kinds of risks are leaders likely to take?

Genesis 12:1 *Then the Lord told Abram, "Leave your country, your relatives, and your father's house, and go to the land that I will show you."*

Exodus 3:10 *Now go, for I am sending you to Pharaoh. You will lead my people, the Israelites, out of Egypt.*

Exodus 14:21 *Then Moses raised his hand over the sea, and the Lord opened up a path through the water with a strong east wind.*
Leaders are risk takers. Great things do not happen without risk.

Numbers 14:6-9 *Two of the men who had explored the land, Joshua son of Nun and Caleb son of Jephunneh, tore their clothing. They said to the community of Israel, ". . . Do not rebel against the Lord, and don't be afraid of the people of the land. They are only helpless prey to us! They have no protection, but the Lord is with us! Don't be afraid of them!"*
Leaders risk their resources, their reputations, and even their closest relationships (if that is required) to be faithful to God. The only thing more risky than trusting God is not trusting him!

1 Kings 18:36-37 *At the customary time for offering the evening sacrifice, Elijah the prophet walked up to the altar and prayed, "O Lord, God of Abraham, Isaac, and*

Jacob, prove today that you are God in Israel and that I am your servant. Prove that I have done all this at your command. O Lord, answer me!"
Leaders may be called to take risks that will display the glory of God. You need to be certain you are following God, as with all risks, or else you can make a mockery of your faith and harm others. But when God's call is clear, the wonders are beyond comparison.

Luke 1:38 *Mary responded, "I am the Lord's servant, and I am willing to accept whatever he wants. May everything you have said come true." And then the angel left.*
Leaders often risk rejection and the loss of their security.

Luke 5:4-6 *When he had finished speaking, he said to Simon, "Now go out where it is deeper and let down your nets, and you will catch many fish." "Master," Simon replied, "we worked hard all last night and didn't catch a thing. But if you say so, we'll try again." And this time their nets were so full they began to tear!*
Leaders risk what may appear to be foolish or contrary to their experience because they feel led by the Lord. Such risks, done in obedience, often yield rich rewards.

Luke 5:10-11 *Jesus replied to Simon, "Don't be afraid! From now on you'll be fishing for people!" And as soon as they landed, they left everything and followed Jesus.*
Leaders risk doing the right thing, even when it is the hardest thing.

PROMISE FROM GOD 1 Corinthians 15:58
So, my dear brothers and sisters, be strong and steady, always enthusiastic about the Lord's work, for you know that nothing you do for the Lord is ever useless.

SABBATH

See also **BURNOUT, STRESS, TIME, WORSHIP**

Why should leaders care about Sabbath and rest?

Exodus 20:8-10 *Remember to observe the Sabbath day by keeping it holy. Six days a week are set apart for your daily duties and regular work, but the seventh day is a day of rest dedicated to the Lord your God. On that day no one in your household may do any kind of work. This includes you.*

Exodus 23:12 *Work for six days, and rest on the seventh. This will . . . allow the people of your household . . . to be refreshed.*

Leaders should be concerned to honor God with their time. In the midst of the debate over specific ways to keep the Sabbath, the primary principle is to take time away from the pressures of business so that you can honor the Lord in worship and renew your spirit in spiritual instruction, renewal, and rest.

What are the benefits of taking Sabbath time?

Exodus 31:12-17 *The Lord then gave these further instructions to Moses: "Tell the people of Israel to keep my Sabbath day, for the Sabbath is a sign of the covenant between me and you forever. It helps you to remember that I am the Lord, who makes you holy. . . . It is a permanent sign of my covenant with them. For in six days the Lord made heaven and earth, but he rested on the seventh day and was refreshed."*

It isn't enough for leaders to just "get something done." God's people are to do God's work God's way. It's important to remember that the Sabbath principle was given at the same time as the building of the tabernacle. In the midst of the holy urgency to construct the place of worship, the people were commanded to remember above all else the place of the Sabbath in the pace of their lives. From the outset, God warned against the fallacy that religious effort should replace obedience to God. The Sabbath principle reveals God's design for the rhythm of life.

Mark 6:30-31 *The apostles returned to Jesus from their ministry tour and told him all they had done and what they had taught. Then Jesus said, "Let's get away from the crowds for a while and rest." There were so many people coming and going that Jesus and his apostles didn't even have time to eat.*

Leaders value rest, especially after hard work. Rest is not only for the recovery of energy, but also for the savoring of the work everyone has completed. The irony of this passage is that the disciples were not able to rest immediately because the crowds followed them. Their rest was delayed but not forgotten. Though forces and demands will conspire against your rest, you must continually make it your goal to pursue a holy pace.

Isaiah 58:13 *Keep the Sabbath day holy. Don't pursue your own interests on that day, but enjoy the Sabbath and speak of it with delight as the Lord's holy day.*

Mark 2:27 *He said to them, "The Sabbath was made to benefit people, and not people to benefit the Sabbath."*

God gave Sabbath rest to his people for his honor as well as for their welfare and delight. When you take time for Sabbath, you take time to remind yourself that while you have many responsibilities in this world, you live for the next world.

PROMISE FROM GOD Hebrews 4:9-10 *There is a special rest still waiting for the people of God. For all who enter into God's rest will find rest from their labors, just as God rested after creating the world.*

SELF-DISCIPLINE

See **PERSONAL DISCIPLINE**

SELF-ESTEEM

What makes me, as a leader, valuable and important?
Romans 8:15-17 *So you should not be like cowering, fearful slaves. You should behave instead like God's very own children, adopted into his family—calling him "Father, dear Father." For his Holy Spirit speaks to us deep in our hearts and tells us that we are God's children. And since we are his children, we will share his treasures—for everything God gives to his Son, Christ, is ours, too.*
Leaders are tempted to measure their value on the basis of performance or other external measurements. But your worth is rooted in the fact that you are created in God's image and loved as God's child. These truths affect not only how you view yourself, but also how you view those you lead.

Jeremiah 1:5 *I knew you before I formed you in your mother's womb. Before you were born I set you apart and appointed you as my spokesman to the world.*
God made you with great skill, crafting you with loving care. God showed how much value he places on you by the way he made you.

Psalm 139:1-3, 6 *O Lord, you have examined my heart and know everything about me. You know when I sit*

down or stand up. You know my every thought when far away. You chart the path ahead of me and tell me where to stop and rest. Every moment you know where I am. . . . Such knowledge is too wonderful for me!
God values you so much that he watches over you no matter where you are or what you are doing. This truly is wonderful, too wonderful to claim. But it tells you how special he thinks you are.

1 Corinthians 6:19 *Or don't you know that your body is the temple of the Holy Spirit, who lives in you and was given to you by God?*
God values people so much that he indwells those who believe, so that our bodies are temples. Therefore you are to honor him with your body.

How do I develop a healthy self-esteem?
Romans 12:3 *Be honest in your estimate of yourselves, measuring your value by how much faith God has given you.*
Healthy self-esteem is an honest appraisal of yourself, not too proud because of the gifts and abilities God has given you, yet not so self-effacing that you fail to use your gifts and abilities to their potential.

1 Peter 4:10 *God has given gifts to each of you. . . . Manage them well so that God's generosity can flow through you.*
Giving actually increases your sense of self-worth because it allows God to work more effectively through you.

PROMISE FROM GOD Matthew 10:29-31 *Not even a sparrow, worth only half a penny, can fall to the ground without your Father knowing it. . . . You are more valuable to him than a whole flock of sparrows.*

SERVANTHOOD

See also **AUTHORITY, GREATNESS, HUMILITY, POWER**

How are leaders to view themselves?

Matthew 20:26 *Whoever wants to be a leader among you must be your servant.*

Mark 10:45 *For even I, the Son of Man, came here not to be served but to serve others.*
The biblical model for leadership is servanthood. Worldly leaders use power to get things done for themselves, but godly leaders use power to serve those they are called to lead and care for. Worldly leaders want to be served; godly leaders want to serve.

What does it mean for me to be a servant leader?

John 13:4-5, 14-15 *So he got up from the table, took off his robe, wrapped a towel around his waist, and poured water into a basin. Then he began to wash the disciples' feet and to wipe them with the towel he had around him. . . . "And since I, the Lord and Teacher, have washed your feet, you ought to wash each other's feet. I have given you an example to follow. Do as I have done to you."*
Jesus revolutionizes our understanding of leadership by teaching "downward mobility." In a most striking picture of servanthood, Jesus humbles himself through obedience. By performing the task of a slave, Jesus models how far you are to go in serving others.

Matthew 20:32 *Jesus stopped in the road and called, "What do you want me to do for you?"*
Servant leaders listen and respond to the needs of those around them.

How can I develop a servant heart?

Philippians 2:5-7 *Your attitude should be the same that Christ Jesus had. Though he was God, he did not demand and cling to his rights as God. He made himself nothing; he took the humble position of a slave and appeared in human form.*
Humbling yourself as Christ did will help you to obediently do what God wants.

Romans 6:13 *And use your whole body as a tool to do what is right for the glory of God.*
Submit yourself to Christ and remain pure.

Genesis 24:18-20 *"Certainly, sir," she said, and she quickly lowered the jug for him to drink. When he had finished, she said, "I'll draw water for your camels, too, until they have had enough!" So she quickly emptied the jug into the watering trough and ran down to the well again. She kept carrying water to the camels until they had finished drinking.*
Helping others cultivates a servant's heart.

Luke 1:38 *Mary responded, "I am the Lord's servant, and I am willing to accept whatever he wants. May everything you have said come true." And then the angel left.*
The essence of servant leadership is doing what God asks you to do.

PROMISES FROM GOD Matthew 16:25 *If you give up your life for me, you will find true life.*

Mark 10:43-44 *But among you it should be quite different. Whoever wants to be a leader among you must be your servant, and whoever wants to be first must be the slave of all.*

SETBACKS

See also **PERSEVERANCE, TRIALS/TROUBLE**

How do leaders keep going in the face of setbacks?

Genesis 37:28 *So when the traders came by, his brothers pulled Joseph out of the pit and sold him for twenty pieces of silver, and the Ishmaelite traders took him along to Egypt.*

Genesis 39:19-20 *After hearing his wife's story, Potiphar was furious! He took Joseph and threw him into the prison where the king's prisoners were held.*

Genesis 40:23 *Pharaoh's cup-bearer, however, promptly forgot all about Joseph, never giving him another thought.*

Leaders must expect setbacks. We live in a fallen world with fallen people. No story more vividly illustrates the principles for dealing with setbacks than the story of Joseph, the son of Jacob, as told in Genesis. In spite of his dreams about greatness, he experienced setbacks by being sold into slavery by his brothers, being framed as a rapist by Potiphar's wife, and being forgotten by the cup-bearer whose dream Joseph had properly interpreted. How did Joseph deal with these setbacks, which would have overwhelmed most of us?

Genesis 50:19-20 *But Joseph told them, "Don't be afraid of me. Am I God, to judge and punish you? As far as I am concerned, God turned into good what you meant for evil. He brought me to the high position I have today so I could save the lives of many people."*

Leaders look beyond the immediate crises to the eventual fulfillment. Joseph knew by faith that God would keep his word, so Joseph wasn't discouraged by the delays, setbacks, and detours. This kept him free of bitterness and resentment.

1 Samuel 24:10 *For the Lord placed you at my mercy back there in the cave, and some of my men told me to kill you, but I spared you. For I said, "I will never harm him—he is the Lord's anointed one."*
Leaders endure setbacks by trusting God's timing. David, though anointed as a youth to become king, faced continual setbacks as Saul hunted him down. Yet David refused to take matters into his own hands by killing Saul. He knew God would deal with Saul in God's own time and way.

Acts 16:6-10 *Next Paul and Silas traveled through the area of Phrygia and Galatia, because the Holy Spirit had told them not to go into the province of Asia at that time. Then coming to the borders of Mysia, they headed for the province of Bithynia, but again the Spirit of Jesus did not let them go. So instead, they went on through Mysia to the city of Troas. That night Paul had a vision. He saw a man from Macedonia in northern Greece, pleading with him, "Come over here and help us." So we decided to leave for Macedonia at once, for we could only conclude that God was calling us to preach the Good News there.*
Leaders learn that when God closes some doors, he almost always opens others.

PROMISE FROM GOD
Hebrews 10:36 *Patient endurance is what you need now, so you will continue to do God's will. Then you will receive all that he has promised.*

SPIRITUAL DISCIPLINES

See also **BALANCE, PERSONAL DISCIPLINE, PRAYER**

How does a leader maintain spiritual vitality?

Proverbs 4:23 *Above all else, guard your heart, for it affects everything you do.*
A leader leads from the heart. The actual Hebrew for this phrase says "Above all else, guard your heart, *for from it flow the springs of life*" (italics added, italic phrase NASB). Every aspect of life is controlled by the spiritual condition of your heart. Because of the impact leaders can make, you, above all, must care for your inner life. The spiritual disciplines are the ways you care for your heart and soul. Because they nurture and strengthen your inner life, these disciplines are also called "spiritual exercises." Some of the classic spiritual disciplines include: Bible study and meditation, prayer, fasting, silence, solitude, worship, stewardship, repentance and confession, service, and spiritual direction (discerning God's presence and will in your life). The spiritual disciplines are not practiced to impress God, but rather to allow God to impress himself on you. They are not achievements you perform for God, but ways you make yourself available to God.

1 Corinthians 9:27 *I discipline my body like an athlete, training it to do what it should. Otherwise, I fear that after preaching to others I myself might be disqualified.*
As an athlete trains over and over again so that fundamental actions become almost automatic, so leaders discipline themselves to develop spiritual reflexes.

1 Timothy 4:7-8 *Spend your time and energy in training yourself for spiritual fitness. Physical exercise has*

some value, but spiritual exercise is much more important, for it promises a reward in both this life and the next. Leaders take the long view. That's why they take time for spiritual development and conditioning. Spirituality prepares you not only for this life, but also develops your heart and soul more fully for eternity.

PROMISE FROM GOD Jeremiah 29:13 *If you look for me in earnest, you will find me when you seek me.*

SPIRITUAL DRYNESS

See **BURNOUT, DISCOURAGEMENT, SABBATH**

SPIRITUAL WARFARE

See also **TEMPTATION**

Is spiritual warfare a reality?

Genesis 3:1 *Now the serpent was the shrewdest of all the creatures the Lord God had made. "Really?" he asked the woman. "Did God really say you must not eat any of the fruit in the garden?"*

Matthew 4:1 *Then Jesus was led out into the wilderness by the Holy Spirit to be tempted there by the Devil.* From the beginning of time and from the beginning of Jesus' own ministry, the Bible clearly teaches that human beings are involved in a spiritual battle. Far from excluding us from spiritual battles, faith puts us right in the midst of them. Leaders who fail to take account of this put themselves and those they lead in jeopardy.

How does the spiritual battle affect leaders?

John 8:44 *The Devil . . . was a murderer from the beginning and has always hated the truth. There is no truth in him. When he lies, it is consistent with his character; for he is a liar and the father of lies.*

Satan's first tactic is to distort God's Word. If he can raise suspicion about the integrity of God's Word, he can get you to question God's will and intentions for you. Leaders must know God's Word and recognize the lies that most often come in the guise of cultural mores and worldviews.

1 Chronicles 21:1 *Satan rose up against Israel and caused David to take a census of the Israelites.*

Leaders are often tempted to rely on their own resources—on the tangible, measurable assets they can count. While it is wise to understand your resources, it is unwise to think that your ultimate security is in them. David's census was an unholy inventory of his military might that was in direct contradiction to David's experience of God's provision and protection throughout his lifetime.

Matthew 4:3-9 *Then the Devil came and said to him, "If you are the Son of God, change these stones into loaves of bread." . . . Then the Devil took him to Jerusalem, to the highest point of the Temple, and said, "If you are the Son of God, jump off!" . . . Next the Devil took him to the peak of a very high mountain and showed him the nations of the world and all their glory. "I will give it all to you," he said, "if you will only kneel down and worship me."*

In the spiritual battle, leaders are often tempted by offers of personal gain, pride, and overconfidence.

How do I fight the spiritual battle?

Matthew 4:4 *But Jesus told him, "No! The Scriptures say . . ."*

Psalm 119:11 *I have hidden your word in my heart, that I might not sin against you.*
The best defense against Satan's lies is God's truth.

Ephesians 6:10-18 *A final word: Be strong with the Lord's mighty power. Put on all of God's armor so that you will be able to stand firm against all strategies and tricks of the Devil. For we are not fighting against people made of flesh and blood, but against the evil rulers and authorities of the unseen world, against those mighty powers of darkness who rule this world, and against wicked spirits in the heavenly realms. Use every piece of God's armor to resist the enemy in the time of evil, so that after the battle you will still be standing firm. Stand your ground, putting on the sturdy belt of truth and the body armor of God's righteousness. For shoes, put on the peace that comes from the Good News, so that you will be fully prepared. In every battle you will need faith as your shield to stop the fiery arrows aimed at you by Satan. Put on salvation as your helmet, and take the sword of the Spirit, which is the word of God. Pray at all times and on every occasion in the power of the Holy Spirit. Stay alert and be persistent in your prayers for all Christians everywhere.*
Warfare prayer is a matter of claiming your authority in Christ. Stand your ground in the power of the gospel, confident in the victory of Christ. Leaders see beyond the human antagonists to the spiritual enemy, often working through the unaware parties involved. Godly leaders prepare themselves with the resources Paul enumerates, depending on God's protection, not their own intellect or cleverness.

PROMISE FROM GOD Ephesians 6:11 *Put on all of God's armor so that you will be able to stand firm against all strategies and tricks of the Devil.*

STATUS/IMAGE

See **PRIDE**

STEWARDSHIP

See also **ABILITIES, MONEY, RESPONSIBILITY**

How do leaders view their responsibilities?

Matthew 24:45-47 *Who is a faithful, sensible servant, to whom the master can give the responsibility of managing his household and feeding his family? If the master returns and finds that the servant has done a good job, there will be a reward. I assure you, the master will put that servant in charge of all he owns.*

Matthew 25:14-15, 29 *Again, the Kingdom of Heaven can be illustrated by the story of a man going on a trip. He called together his servants and gave them money to invest for him while he was gone. He gave five bags of gold to one, two bags of gold to another, and one bag of gold to the last—dividing it in proportion to their abilities. . . . To those who use well what they are given, even more will be given, and they will have an abundance. But from those who are unfaithful, even what little they have will be taken away.*

Luke 12:48 *Much is required from those to whom much is given, and much more is required from those to whom much more is given.*
Leadership is a matter of stewardship. Leaders are ultimately accountable to God for the use of their gifts and opportunities. God entrusts resources to each person and then expects us to maximize the effectiveness of those abilities in wise and godly stewardship. While the most talented leaders may seem the most blessed, they must also be the most responsible.

2 Corinthians 5:9-10 *So our aim is to please him always, whether we are here in this body or away from this body. For we must all stand before Christ to be judged. We will each receive whatever we deserve for the good or evil we have done in our bodies.*
Stewardship means accountability. Wise, godly leaders make their decisions and conduct their lives in the light of eternity.

How should I handle my material resources?
Leviticus 25:23 *Remember, the land must never be sold on a permanent basis because it really belongs to me. You are only foreigners and tenants living with me.*

Psalm 89:11 *The heavens are yours, and the earth is yours; everything in the world is yours—you created it all.*

Proverbs 3:9-10 *Honor the Lord with your wealth and with the best part of everything your land produces. Then he will fill your barns with grain.*
Stewardship begins by acknowledging that the Lord owns everything. Since everything belongs to God, whatever you have is held in trust from God.

Proverbs 11:24-25 *It is possible to give freely and become more wealthy, but those who are stingy will lose everything. The generous prosper and are satisfied; those who refresh others will themselves be refreshed.*

Luke 6:38 *If you give, you will receive.*

2 Corinthians 9:6 *The one who plants generously will get a generous crop.*
You do not give in order to grow richer, but you may grow richer when you give. While it is not always true, one of the reasons is that the qualities that make you generous also make you responsible and trustworthy. But the primary reason is that God, in his grace, may entrust more to you so that you will be a channel of his blessing in this world.

Malachi 3:10 *"Bring all the tithes into the storehouse. . . . If you do," says the Lord Almighty, "I will open the windows of heaven for you."*
You will be held accountable for your use of the blessings God entrusts to you. God honors faithfulness in giving.

PROMISE FROM GOD Psalm 112:5 *All goes well for those who are generous, who lend freely and conduct their business fairly.*

STRESS

See also **BALANCE, BURNOUT, DISCOURAGEMENT, SABBATH**

What are some of the dangers of stress?
Numbers 11:10-15 *Moses was also very aggravated. And Moses said to the Lord, "Why are you treating me, your servant, so miserably? What did I do to deserve the*

burden of a people like this? . . . Where am I supposed to get meat for all these people? They keep complaining and saying, 'Give us meat!' I can't carry all these people by myself! The load is far too heavy! I'd rather you killed me than treat me like this. Please spare me this misery!"

2 Corinthians 1:8-9 *I think you ought to know, dear brothers and sisters, about the trouble we went through in the province of Asia. We were crushed and completely overwhelmed, and we thought we would never live through it. In fact, we expected to die.*

The intense demands that leaders experience can be overwhelming. The expectations, the criticism, the scope of the need and responsibility can threaten to crush even the strongest leader.

Luke 10:40-41 *But Martha was worrying over the big dinner she was preparing. She came to Jesus and said, "Lord, doesn't it seem unfair to you that my sister just sits here while I do all the work? Tell her to come and help me." But the Lord said to her, "My dear Martha, you are so upset over all these details!"*

Matthew 13:22 *The thorny ground represents those who hear and accept the Good News, but all too quickly the message is crowded out by the cares of this life and the lure of wealth, so no crop is produced.*

Stress can cause you to focus on the unimportant and miss the important. As pressure squeezes your perspective inward, you lose your perspective outward. Preoccupation with the trivia of the moment blinds you to the big picture.

How can I deal with stress and pressure?

2 Corinthians 4:8-10 *We are pressed on every side by troubles, but we are not crushed and broken. We are perplexed, but we don't give up and quit. We are hunted*

down, but God never abandons us. We get knocked down, but we get up again and keep going. Through suffering, these bodies of ours constantly share in the death of Jesus so that the life of Jesus may also be seen in our bodies.

No matter what the source of stress, your source of strength must be the Lord.

Psalm 55:22 *Give your burdens to the Lord, and he will take care of you. He will not permit the godly to slip and fall.*

Psalm 62:2 *He alone is my rock and my salvation, my fortress where I will never be shaken.*

Psalm 86:7 *I will call to you whenever trouble strikes, and you will answer me.*

Isaiah 41:10 *Don't be afraid, for I am with you. Do not be dismayed, for I am your God. I will strengthen you. I will help you. I will uphold you with my victorious right hand.*

John 14:1 *Don't be troubled. You trust God, now trust in me.*

God's availability and promises provide the most effective stress reducers of all.

Is stress ever positive?

James 1:2-4 *Dear brothers and sisters, whenever trouble comes your way, let it be an opportunity for joy. For when your faith is tested, your endurance has a chance to grow. So let it grow, for when your endurance is fully developed, you will be strong in character and ready for anything.*

Romans 5:3-4 *We can rejoice, too, when we run into problems and trials, for we know that they are good for us—they help us learn to endure. And endurance develops strength of character in us, and character strengthens our confident expectation of salvation.*

Stress and pressure can both test and develop strength of character. The question is not whether or not you will have stress, but what you will do with it when it comes. If you deal with stress and pressure with your own strength, you may be quickly and easily overcome. If you let God help you deal with your pressure, you can come out stronger and more joyful.

PROMISE FROM GOD John 16:33 *I have told you all this so that you may have peace in me. Here on earth you will have many trials and sorrows. But take heart, because I have overcome the world.*

SUCCESS

See also **ACHIEVEMENTS**

What is the biblical measure of success?

John 17:3 *And this is the way to have eternal life—to know you, the only true God, and Jesus Christ, the one you sent to earth.*

Matthew 22:37-38 *Jesus replied, "'You must love the Lord your God with all your heart, all your soul, and all your mind.' This is the first and greatest commandment."*
Success is knowing God. Technically, this is not something you achieve for yourself, but it is at the heart of life.

2 Corinthians 5:9-10 *So our aim is to please him always, whether we are here in this body or away from this body. For we must all stand before Christ to be judged. We will each receive whatever we deserve for the good or evil we have done in our bodies.*
Success is pleasing God. Leaders take their agenda from

God. Their goals are ultimately rooted in what they can achieve with integrity and with ways consistent with loving God and others. No matter what you do, you can conduct your life in ways that will honor and please God.

John 15:8, 16 *My true disciples produce much fruit. This brings great glory to my Father. . . . You didn't choose me. I chose you. I appointed you to go and produce fruit that will last, so that the Father will give you whatever you ask for, using my name.*

Philippians 1:22 *Yet if I live, that means fruitful service for Christ.*
Success is bearing fruit for God. Fruit is the product of abiding in Christ. As you abide in the vine, the vine bears fruit through you. The fruit comes as a result of your relationship in the vine, not your focusing on the fruit. Success, therefore, is a by-product of faithfulness.

What are the dangers of living for worldly success?
Genesis 13:10-13 *Lot took a long look at the fertile plains of the Jordan Valley in the direction of Zoar. The whole area was well watered everywhere, like the garden of the Lord or the beautiful land of Egypt. (This was before the Lord had destroyed Sodom and Gomorrah.) Lot chose that land for himself—the Jordan Valley to the east of them. He went there with his flocks and servants and parted company with his uncle Abram. So while Abram stayed in the land of Canaan, Lot moved his tents to a place near Sodom, among the cities of the plain. The people of this area were unusually wicked and sinned greatly against the Lord.*
Leaders may be seduced by appearances and miss the rot beneath. Lot chose the fertile valley of Sodom, not caring that its people were wicked. It would later cost him his family—and other dreadful consequences.

Luke 9:25 *And how do you benefit if you gain the whole world but lose or forfeit your own soul in the process?*

Luke 12:16-21 *And he gave an illustration: "A rich man had a fertile farm that produced fine crops. In fact, his barns were full to overflowing. So he said, 'I know! I'll tear down my barns and build bigger ones. Then I'll have room enough to store everything. And I'll sit back and say to myself, My friend, you have enough stored away for years to come. Now take it easy! Eat, drink, and be merry!' But God said to him, 'You fool! You will die this very night. Then who will get it all?' Yes, a person is a fool to store up earthly wealth but not have a rich relationship with God."*
The greatest danger is being a success in the world and an absolute failure with God. To gain the world and lose your soul is the ultimate failure.

Mark 4:19 *But all too quickly the message is crowded out by the cares of this life, the lure of wealth, and the desire for nice things.*
Attraction to worldly things can smother the success that comes from God. When you lust for money, position, power, or fame, you will be tempted to spend your energies to get these things, and that will take you away from a pursuit of God.

How do I keep my focus on godly success?
Matthew 6:19-21 *Don't store up treasures here on earth, where they can be eaten by moths and get rusty, and where thieves break in and steal. Store your treasures in heaven, where they will never become moth-eaten or rusty and where they will be safe from thieves. Wherever your treasure is, there your heart and thoughts will also be.*
Deliberately put your treasures with God so that your heart follows. This means that you must set priorities and measure accomplishments by biblical standards,

not worldly criteria. Godly leaders will not ignore worldly standards, but they keep them in perspective.

1 Timothy 4:7-8 *Spend your time and energy in training yourself for spiritual fitness. Physical exercise has some value, but spiritual exercise is much more important, for it promises a reward in both this life and the next.* Spiritual fitness keeps you focused for spiritual success.

Philippians 3:12-14 *But I keep working toward that day when I will finally be all that Christ Jesus saved me for and wants me to be. No, dear brothers and sisters, I am still not all I should be, but I am focusing all my energies on this one thing: Forgetting the past and looking forward to what lies ahead, I strain to reach the end of the race and receive the prize for which God, through Christ Jesus, is calling us up to heaven.*

2 Timothy 4:6-8 *The time of my death is near. I have fought a good fight, I have finished the race, and I have remained faithful. And now the prize awaits me—the crown of righteousness that the Lord, the righteous Judge, will give me on that great day of his return. And the prize is not just for me but for all who eagerly look forward to his glorious return.*
Constant awareness of your heavenly rewards helps you be constant in faithfulness.

Is it okay to try to be successful in this life?
Proverbs 12:24 *Work hard and become a leader; be lazy and become a slave.*

Proverbs 22:29 *Do you see any truly competent workers? They will serve kings rather than ordinary people.* Many godly character traits (such as hard work, integrity, commitment, serving others, planning), if applied to life, often bring material success.

Genesis 39:2-3 *The Lord was with Joseph and blessed him greatly as he served in the home of his Egyptian master . . . , giving him success in everything he did.*

Job 42:12 *So the Lord blessed Job in the second half of his life even more than in the beginning.*

Throughout the Scriptures, there are frequent references to God's blessings for his people. God allows his people to have material blessing, but urges them never to sacrifice spiritual matters for worldly wealth.

PROMISE FROM GOD Psalm 84:11 *For the Lord God is our light and protector. He gives us grace and glory. No good thing will the Lord withhold from those who do what is right.*

SUFFERING

See **SETBACKS, TRIALS/TROUBLE**

TALENT

See **ABILITIES**

TEAMWORK

See **DELEGATION, ORGANIZATION, PARTNERSHIP**

TEMPER

See **ANGER**

TEMPTATION

See also **INTEGRITY, SPIRITUAL WARFARE**

What kinds of temptations do leaders face?

2 Samuel 11:1-2 *The following spring, the time of year when kings go to war, David sent Joab and the Israelite army to destroy the Ammonites. In the process they laid siege to the city of Rabbah. But David stayed behind in Jerusalem. Late one afternoon David got out of bed after taking a nap and went for a stroll on the roof of the palace. As he looked out over the city, he noticed a woman of unusual beauty taking a bath.*

A leader faces particular temptations, especially when everything is going well. David had reached the place where he could enjoy an amount of freedom because he had won many battles and had a trusted leadership team in place. But there are other battlefronts where no one else can fight for you.

1 Kings 11:1-4 *Now King Solomon loved many foreign women. . . . The Lord had clearly instructed his people not to intermarry with those nations, because the women they married would lead them to worship their gods. Yet Solomon insisted on loving them anyway. . . . And sure enough, they led his heart away from the Lord. In Solomon's old age, they turned his heart to worship their gods instead of trusting only in the Lord his God, as his father, David, had done.*

Leaders are tempted to think they are special and that they are exempt from the standards that apply to everyone else. But because leaders are human, they are subject to the same weaknesses as everyone else.

2 Chronicles 26:14-16 *Uzziah provided the entire army with shields, spears, helmets, coats of mail,*

bows, and sling stones. And he produced machines mounted on the walls of Jerusalem, designed by brilliant men to shoot arrows and hurl stones from the towers and the corners of the wall. His fame spread far and wide, for the Lord helped him wonderfully until he became very powerful. But when he had become powerful, he also became proud, which led to his downfall.

The very achievements that God allows and enables can make you vulnerable to temptation. Uzziah's success led to the presumption that he had the authority to do anything. This caused him to sin when he offered incense that God said only a priest could offer.

John 12:4-6 *But Judas Iscariot, one of his disciples—the one who would betray him—said, "That perfume was worth a small fortune. It should have been sold and the money given to the poor." Not that he cared for the poor—he was a thief who was in charge of the disciples' funds, and he often took some for his own use.*

Leaders are tempted to take advantage of the trust given them.

Numbers 20:7-12 *The Lord said to Moses, "You and Aaron must take the staff and assemble the entire community. As the people watch, command the rock over there to pour out its water. You will get enough water from the rock to satisfy all the people and their livestock." So Moses did as he was told. He took the staff from the place where it was kept before the Lord. Then he and Aaron summoned the people to come and gather at the rock. "Listen, you rebels!" he shouted. "Must we bring you water from this rock?" Then Moses raised his hand and struck the rock twice with the staff, and water gushed out. So all the people and their livestock drank their fill. But the Lord said to Moses and Aaron, "Because you did not trust me enough*

to demonstrate my holiness to the people of Israel, you will not lead them into the land I am giving them!"
Leaders are often tempted to be frustrated and angry with those they lead. Moses gave in to his anger with the people and forfeited the opportunity to lead them into the Promised Land.

How can I avoid falling into temptation?
Genesis 39:12 *He ran from the house.*

Proverbs 1:10 *If sinners entice you, turn your back on them!*
Flee the situation when at all possible. You also should stay away from the influences of people you know are trying to bring you down.

Daniel 1:8 *But Daniel made up his mind not to defile himself by eating the food.*
Commit to refusing temptation. A solid commitment made before temptation strikes is the best preventive to sin.

Matthew 6:13 *And don't let us yield to temptation.*
Make your temptations a constant focus of prayer.

Psalm 1:1 *Oh, the joys of those who do not follow the advice of the wicked.*

Titus 2:12 *And we are instructed to turn from godless living and sinful pleasures.*
Continue to grow spiritually. Christian growth brings an increased awareness and sensitivity to temptation in your life.

1 Corinthians 10:13 *But remember that the temptations that come into your life are no different from what others experience. And God is faithful. He will keep the temptation from becoming so strong that you can't stand*

up against it. When you are tempted, he will show you a way out so that you will not give in to it.
Look for the way out. God has promised that he will provide a way of escape from temptation.

PROMISE FROM GOD 2 Thessalonians 3:3
But the Lord is faithful; he will make you strong and guard you from the evil one.

TIME

See also **BALANCE, MOTIVATION, PERSONAL DISCIPLINE, SABBATH**

How do leaders view their time?

Psalm 90:12 *Teach us to make the most of our time, so that we may grow in wisdom.*
Time is a gift. Leaders are stewards not only of their own time, but also of the time of others who work in the organization and who are served by the organization. They want to utilize time to the fullest.

Ecclesiastes 3:1, 11 *There is a time for everything, a season for every activity under heaven. . . . God has made everything beautiful for its own time. He has planted eternity in the human heart, but even so, people cannot see the whole scope of God's work from beginning to end.*
Leaders trust that they don't have to force things to happen. They learn to depend on God's timing.

PROMISE FROM GOD Ephesians 5:15-16
So be careful how you live, not as fools but as those who are wise. Make the most of every opportunity for doing good in these evil days.

TITHING

See **MONEY, STEWARDSHIP**

TRAINING

See **DELEGATION, MENTORING**

TRIALS/TROUBLE

See also **CRISIS, PERSEVERANCE, SETBACKS**

What causes trials and trouble in life?

Genesis 3:17-19 *I have placed a curse on the ground. All your life you will struggle to scratch a living from it. It will grow thorns and thistles for you, though you will eat of its grains. All your life you will sweat to produce food, until your dying day. Then you will return to the ground from which you came. For you were made from dust, and to the dust you will return.*

John 16:33 *I have told you all this so that you may have peace in me. Here on earth you will have many trials and sorrows. But take heart, because I have overcome the world.*

We live in a fallen world and expect there to be troubles. But along with the troubles comes the strength and wisdom of God to handle them.

Psalm 51:4 *Against you, and you alone, have I sinned; I have done what is evil in your sight. You will be proved right in what you say, and your judgment against me is just.*

Proverbs 12:13 *The wicked are trapped by their own words, but the godly escape such trouble.*
Trouble is often the result of our own poor decisions and sin.

Jonah 1:3-4 *But Jonah got up and went in the opposite direction in order to get away from the Lord. . . . He found a ship leaving for Tarshish. . . . Suddenly the Lord flung a powerful wind over the sea.*
We can expect to find ourselves in deep trouble if we insist on running away from God, refusing to obey his will.

Psalm 62:3-4 *So many enemies against one man—all of them trying to kill me. . . . They delight in telling lies about me.*
Trouble is sometimes undeserved or caused by others.

How should I respond to trials and troubles?
Psalm 18:6 *But in my distress I cried out to the Lord. . . . He heard me from his sanctuary.*

Psalm 46:1-2 *God is our refuge and strength, always ready to help in times of trouble. So we will not fear, even if earthquakes come and the mountains crumble into the sea.*

Mark 6:48 *He saw that they were in serious trouble. . . . He came to them.*
Leaders are quick to call on the Lord because he makes his power available to those who seek him. Peace, assurance, and rest come not from your efforts and activity, but in stillness before God.

1 Peter 1:6-7 *So be truly glad! There is wonderful joy ahead, even though it is necessary for you to endure many trials for a while. These trials are only to test your faith, to show that it is strong and pure. It is being tested as fire tests and purifies gold—and your faith is far more*

precious to God than mere gold. So if your faith remains strong after being tried by fiery trials, it will bring you much praise and glory and honor on the day when Jesus Christ is revealed to the whole world.
Adversity is the true test of leadership. In fact, adversity is the fire that refines and the hammer that shapes a leader. Adversity reveals your shortcomings and drives you to seek God's wisdom and power.

James 1:2-4 *Dear brothers and sisters, whenever trouble comes your way, let it be an opportunity for joy. For when your faith is tested, your endurance has a chance to grow. So let it grow, for when your endurance is fully developed, you will be strong in character and ready for anything.*
Your trials often deepen your ability to lead. They refine your vision of God, clarify your priorities, strip away the illusions of life, reveal God's grace and comfort, and keep you humble.

Galatians 6:2 *Share each other's troubles and problems, and in this way obey the law of Christ.*
Trials drive you into fellowship with others, building community by breaking down the barriers of self-reliance and isolation that so easily tempt a leader.

2 Chronicles 20:12 *O our God, won't you stop them? We are powerless against this mighty army that is about to attack us. We do not know what to do, but we are looking to you for help.*
Troubles teach you to rely on God's provision.

What are some common mistakes I might make in handling problems?

Job 10:18-19 *Why, then, did you bring me out of my mother's womb? Why didn't you let me die at birth?*

Then I would have been spared this miserable existence. I would have gone directly from the womb to the grave.
Doubting God's work in your life. When you begin to doubt God's work, you begin to doubt God.

Genesis 16:1-2 *But Sarai, Abram's wife, had no children. So Sarai took her servant, an Egyptian woman named Hagar, and gave her to Abram so she could bear his children. "The LORD has kept me from having any children," Sarai said to Abram. "Go and sleep with my servant. Perhaps I can have children through her."*
Impatiently taking matters into your own hands instead of allowing God to work his way in his time.

Genesis 3:12-13 *"Yes," Adam admitted, "but it was the woman you gave me who brought me the fruit, and I ate it." Then the Lord God asked the woman, "How could you do such a thing?" "The serpent tricked me," she replied. "That's why I ate it."*

Genesis 16:5 *Then Sarai said to Abram, "It's all your fault! Now this servant of mine is pregnant, and she despises me, though I myself gave her the privilege of sleeping with you. The Lord will make you pay for doing this to me!"*
Blaming others for your self-inflicted problem and even your self-inflicted failed solution.

Numbers 13:25-28 *After exploring the land for forty days, the men returned to Moses. . . . This was their report to Moses: "We arrived in the land you sent us to see, and it is indeed a magnificent country—a land flowing with milk and honey. . . . But the people living there are powerful, and their cities and towns are fortified and very large. We also saw the descendants of Anak who are living there!"*
Focusing too much on the negative possibilities of

what might happen rather than the positive potential of what God can do.

Genesis 16:8 *The angel said to her, "Hagar, Sarai's servant, where have you come from, and where are you going?" "I am running away from my mistress," she replied.* Yielding to the temptation to run away from your problems.

PROMISES FROM GOD Romans 8:28 *And we know that God causes everything to work together for the good of those who love God and are called according to his purpose for them.*

Psalm 54:6-7 *I will praise your name, O Lord, for it is good. For you will rescue me from my troubles and help me to triumph over my enemies.*

Psalm 86:7 *I will call to you whenever trouble strikes, and you will answer me.*

Psalm 50:15 *Trust me in your times of trouble, and I will rescue you, and you will give me glory.*

TRUST

See **CHARACTER, INTEGRITY**

TRUSTWORTHINESS

See **CHARACTER**

UNEMPLOYMENT

See **APPROVAL, PROVISION, SELF-ESTEEM**

VISION

See also **GOALS, MOTIVATION**

How is vision essential to leadership?

Ephesians 3:20 *Now glory be to God! By his mighty power at work within us, he is able to accomplish infinitely more than we would ever dare to ask or hope.*

John 14:12-14 *The truth is, anyone who believes in me will do the same works I have done, and even greater works, because I am going to be with the Father. You can ask for anything in my name, and I will do it, because the work of the Son brings glory to the Father. Yes, ask anything in my name, and I will do it!*

Vision breaks your bondage to small ideas that are not worthy of God or representative of God's work in the world. Vision inspires hope in greater possibilities.

Genesis 12:1-3 *Then the Lord told Abram, "Leave your country, your relatives, and your father's house, and go to the land that I will show you. I will cause you to become the father of a great nation. I will bless you and make you famous, and I will make you a blessing to others. I will bless those who bless you and curse those who curse you. All the families of the earth will be blessed through you."*

God's strategy has always been to give his people a vision of a new reality. This kind of vision inspires obedience and awakens courage.

Genesis 37:5 *One night Joseph had a dream.*
Vision sustains during the delays in reaching your goals. Joseph never lost hope because he kept God's promise before him.

How can I cultivate vision?

2 Kings 6:17 *Elisha prayed, "O Lord, open his eyes and let him see!" The Lord opened his servant's eyes, and when he looked up, he saw that the hillside around Elisha was filled with horses and chariots of fire.*
Prayer is an essential means for developing spiritual vision.

Isaiah 55:8-9 *"My thoughts are completely different from yours," says the Lord. "And my ways are far beyond anything you could imagine. For just as the heavens are higher than the earth, so are my ways higher than your ways and my thoughts higher than your thoughts."*

Psalm 119:18 *Open my eyes to see the wonderful truths in your law.*
God's Word is the primary source for vision and inspiration.

Acts 10:19-20 *Meanwhile, as Peter was puzzling over the vision, the Holy Spirit said to him, "Three men have come looking for you. Go down and go with them without hesitation. All is well, for I have sent them."*

Acts 13:2-3 *One day as these men were worshiping the Lord and fasting, the Holy Spirit said, "Dedicate Barnabas and Saul for the special work I have for them." So after more fasting and prayer, the men laid their hands on them and sent them on their way.*
Vision comes from the inspiration of the Holy Spirit. Leaders learn to be sensitive to the nudges of the Holy Spirit, responding by faith as he leads.

PROMISES FROM GOD 1 Corinthians 13:12 *Now we see things imperfectly as in a poor mirror, but then we will see everything with perfect clarity.*

Revelation 22:4 *They will see his face.*

VOCATION

See **BUSINESS, CALL OF GOD/CALLING, WORK**

VULNERABILITY

See also **BROKENNESS, WEAKNESSES**

Should leaders be vulnerable and open with those they lead?

2 Chronicles 20:12 *O our God, won't you stop them? We are powerless against this mighty army that is about to attack us. We do not know what to do, but we are looking to you for help.*

Psalm 51:12-14 *Restore to me again the joy of your salvation, and make me willing to obey you. Then I will teach your ways to sinners, and they will return to you. Forgive me for shedding blood, O God who saves; then I will joyfully sing of your forgiveness.*

Matthew 26:36-38 *Then Jesus brought them to an olive grove called Gethsemane, and he said, "Sit here while I go on ahead to pray." He took Peter and Zebedee's two sons, James and John, and he began to be filled with anguish and deep distress. He told them, "My soul is crushed with grief to the point of death. Stay here and watch with me."*

2 Corinthians 1:8 *I think you ought to know, dear brothers and sisters, about the trouble we went through in the province of Asia. We were crushed and completely overwhelmed, and we thought we would never live through it.*
Jehoshaphat, the king of Judah, could not hide the fact from his people that he was overwhelmed by the attack coming against the nation. David's sin of adultery with Bathsheba and his murder of Uriah were made public in a psalm for worship. Jesus' agony in Gethsemane was openly shared with his disciples. And Paul did not hide his despair. The stereotype of the leader is a person who has it all together. The reality is that the leader is a person seeking to be faithful to God in a fallen world.

How should I treat those who are vulnerable?

2 Timothy 3:6-9 *They [false teachers] are the kind who work their way into people's homes and win the confidence of vulnerable women who are burdened with the guilt of sin and controlled by many desires. . . . And these teachers fight the truth. . . . Their minds are depraved, and their faith is counterfeit. But they won't get away with this for long. Someday everyone will recognize what fools they are.*
Do not take advantage of anyone who is vulnerable.

Job 6:14 *One should be kind to a fainting friend.*

Isaiah 58:7 *I want you to share your food with the hungry and to welcome poor wanderers into your homes. Give clothes to those who need them, and do not hide from relatives who need your help.*
Help those who are vulnerable and treat them with mercy, compassion, and kindness.

Psalm 82:4 *Rescue the poor and helpless; deliver them from the grasp of evil people.*

Proverbs 31:9 *Yes, speak up for the poor and helpless, and see that they get justice.*
God wants you to rescue the vulnerable so others will not take advantage of them.

PROMISE FROM GOD Psalm 12:5 *I have seen violence done to the helpless, and I have heard the groans of the poor. Now I will rise up to rescue them, as they have longed for me to do.*

WAITING

Why is waiting a natural factor in leadership?
Deuteronomy 7:22 *The Lord your God will drive those nations out ahead of you little by little. You will not clear them away all at once, for if you did, the wild animals would multiply too quickly for you.*
Leaders understand that delay may the best strategy in the long run. As Israel prepared for the conquest of the Promised Land, God revealed that it would happen more gradually because of the need to preserve the biological ecology of the land. God often leads you to follow the path of progressive victory instead of immediate victory for your own protection.

John 16:12 *Oh, there is so much more I want to tell you, but you can't bear it now.*

Galatians 4:4 *But when the right time came, God sent his Son.*
A second reason for waiting is the work of preparation. This includes God's preparation of you, of others, and of events and circumstances involved.

1 Samuel 16:11-13; 2 Samuel 5:4 *Then Samuel asked, "Are these all the sons you have?" "There is still the youngest," Jesse replied. "But he's out in the fields watching the sheep." "Send for him at once," Samuel said. . . . So Jesse sent for him. He was ruddy and handsome, with pleasant eyes. And the Lord said, "This is the one; anoint him." So as David stood there among his brothers, Samuel took the olive oil he had brought and poured it on David's head. . . . David was thirty years old when he began to reign, and he reigned forty years in all.*
A third reason for waiting is humility. Waiting often exposes pride and impatience. Waiting forces you to let go and to realize that ultimately you are not in control. David was a young boy when he was anointed, yet he did not begin to reign until he was thirty years old. There may have been a significant reason behind the delay. During that time (much of which was spent running for his life from King Saul), David learned humility. He refused to do anything against Saul, the Lord's current chosen leader. He trusted God's timing.

How should I respond in a time of waiting?
Psalm 27:14 *Wait patiently for the Lord. Be brave and courageous. Yes, wait patiently for the Lord.*

Psalm 40:1 *I waited patiently for the Lord to help me, and he turned to me and heard my cry.*
Wait with patience and confidence. Rely on the Lord's reliability and on the evidence of God's faithfulness in the past.

Psalm 37:7 *Be still in the presence of the Lord, and wait patiently for him to act. Don't worry about evil people who prosper or fret about their wicked schemes.*
Let go of competition, comparison, and pride during times of waiting. Know that God will deal with evil in his own time.

Isaiah 40:31 *But those who wait on the Lord will find new strength. They will fly high on wings like eagles. They will run and not grow weary. They will walk and not faint.*
Use the times of waiting for spiritual refreshment.

PROMISE FROM GOD Micah 7:7 *As for me, I look to the Lord for his help. I wait confidently for God to save me, and my God will certainly hear me.*

WEAKNESSES

See also **BROKENNESS, VULNERABILITY**

Do leaders always have to be strong?
2 Corinthians 12:9 *Each time he said, "My gracious favor is all you need. My power works best in your weakness." So now I am glad to boast about my weaknesses, so that the power of Christ may work through me.*
Leaders are not always strong. In fact, the challenges, complexities, and demands of leadership often reveal your weaknesses quickly. But God's wisdom and power are demonstrated most clearly in your weaknesses.

PROMISES FROM GOD Isaiah 41:10 *Don't be afraid, for I am with you. Do not be dismayed, for I am your God. I will strengthen you. I will help you. I will uphold you with my victorious right hand.*

Ephesians 3:20 *Glory be to God! By his mighty power at work within us, he is able to accomplish infinitely more than we would ever dare to ask or hope.*

WEALTH

See **MONEY**

WEARINESS

See **BURNOUT, DISCOURAGEMENT**

WILL OF GOD

See **GOD'S WILL**

WISDOM

See also **COUNSEL/COUNSELORS, DECISIONS**

What is a leader's primary desire?

1 Kings 3:5-9 *That night the Lord appeared to Solomon in a dream, and God said, "What do you want? Ask, and I will give it to you!" Solomon replied, ". . . O Lord my God, now you have made me king instead of my father, David, but I am like a little child who doesn't know his way around. And here I am among your own chosen people, a nation so great they are too numerous to count! Give me an understanding mind so that I can govern your people well and know the difference between right and wrong. For who by himself is able to govern this great nation of yours?"*

Of all the skills, qualities, and capabilities leaders desire, none is higher than wisdom. Leaders are responsible to understand situations, people, and issues. You are called upon to interpret trends, to solve problems, and to suggest solutions. In short, you are responsible not only to think, but also to apply knowledge to life situations. That is wisdom.

How does wisdom enable me to be more effective?

Romans 12:2 *Don't copy the behavior and customs of this world, but let God transform you into a new person by changing the way you think. Then you will know what God wants you to do, and you will know how good and pleasing and perfect his will really is.*
Wisdom enables you to break free from worldly perspectives and strategies so that you can discern God's way and will.

1 Corinthians 1:19 *I will destroy human wisdom and discard their most brilliant ideas.*

2 Corinthians 10:4-5 *We use God's mighty weapons, not mere worldly weapons, to knock down the Devil's strongholds. With these weapons we break down every proud argument that keeps people from knowing God. With these weapons we conquer their rebellious ideas, and we teach them to obey Christ.*
Wisdom guards your mind and helps you develop a biblical worldview that penetrates the deception and distortions of worldly systems of morality and thought.

How do I obtain wisdom?

Job 28:12-13, 21 *But do people know where to find wisdom? Where can they find understanding? No one knows where to find it, for it is not found among the living. . . . For it is hidden from the eyes of all humanity.*
Wisdom is not easy for people to obtain.

Job 28:23-24, 27 *God surely knows where it can be found, for he . . . established it and examined it thoroughly.*
God holds all wisdom in his hands.

Job 28:28 *The fear of the Lord is true wisdom; to forsake evil is real understanding.*
God gives wisdom to those who fear him and forsake evil.

Proverbs 9:10 *Fear of the Lord is the beginning of wisdom. Knowledge of the Holy One results in understanding.*
Wisdom comes from having a relationship with God.

Deuteronomy 4:5-6 *You must obey these laws and regulations. . . . If you obey them carefully, you will display your wisdom and intelligence to the surrounding nations. When they hear about these laws, they will exclaim, "What other nation is as wise and prudent as this!"*
Obedience to God's Word—his commands, laws, and teachings—will make you wise.

1 John 2:27 *But you have received the Holy Spirit, and he lives within you, so you don't need anyone to teach you what is true. For the Spirit teaches you all things, and what he teaches is true—it is not a lie. So continue in what he has taught you, and continue to live in Christ.*
Wisdom comes from the Holy Spirit who dwells within those who believe in Christ.

Proverbs 1:5-6 *Let those who are wise listen to these proverbs and become even wiser. And let those who understand receive guidance by exploring the depth of meaning in these proverbs, parables, wise sayings, and riddles.*

Colossians 3:16 *Let the words of Christ, in all their richness, live in your hearts and make you wise. Use his words to teach and counsel each other.*
Listening to Christ's teachings and obeying his words will give wisdom. Obedience to God's Word—his commands, laws, and teachings—will make you wise.

James 1:5 *If you need wisdom—if you want to know what God wants you to do—ask him, and he will gladly tell you. He will not resent your asking.*

Psalm 25:8-9 *The Lord . . . leads the humble in what is right, teaching them his way.*

Proverbs 3:7 *Don't be impressed with your own wisdom. Instead, fear the Lord and turn your back on evil.*
God gives wisdom and guidance to those who are humble.

Proverbs 8:12, 17 *I, Wisdom, live together with good judgment. I know where to discover knowledge and discernment. . . . I love all who love me. Those who search for me will surely find me.*
Those who seek wisdom will find it.

Proverbs 20:18 *Plans succeed through good counsel; don't go to war without the advice of others.*
Wisdom can be found in the counsel of people who have wisdom.

Does spiritual wisdom guarantee success?
Proverbs 5:1-2 *Pay attention to my wisdom. . . . Then you will learn to be discreet.*
Wisdom more often than not protects the wise from evil.

Matthew 7:24 *Anyone who listens to my teaching and obeys me is wise, like a person who builds a house on solid rock.*

Wisdom allows you to build your life on a firm foundation.

Proverbs 3:5-6 *Trust in the Lord with all your heart; do not depend on your own understanding. Seek his will in all you do, and he will direct your paths.*

Proverbs 3:35 *The wise inherit honor, but fools are put to shame!*

Proverbs 24:5 *A wise man is mightier than a strong man, and a man of knowledge is more powerful than a strong man.*
Wisdom itself does not necessarily guarantee success in worldly terms, but it is the road to spiritual satisfaction and joy.

PROMISE FROM GOD Proverbs 1:23 *Come here and listen to me! I'll pour out the spirit of wisdom upon you and make you wise.*

WITNESSING

See **EVANGELISM**

WORDS

See also **COMMUNICATION**

Do a leader's words really matter?
Psalm 15:1-3 *Who may worship in your sanctuary, Lord? Who may enter your presence on your holy hill? Those who lead blameless lives and do what is right, speak-*

ing the truth from sincere hearts. Those who refuse to slander others or harm their neighbors or speak evil of their friends.

James 1:26 *If you claim to be religious but don't control your tongue, you are just fooling yourself, and your religion is worthless.*
Your words matter to God. Godly leaders know that they cannot have a double standard of speaking one way in church and another way on the job or in the community. Your words show what kind of person you really are.

Proverbs 11:11 *Upright citizens bless a city and make it prosper, but the talk of the wicked tears it apart.*
Your words affect the community at large. Wise leaders know that they can greatly help or hinder their group by what they say or don't say.

Deuteronomy 23:23 *But once you have voluntarily made a vow, be careful to do as you have said, for you have made a vow to the Lord your God.*

Joshua 9:19-20 *The leaders replied, "We have sworn an oath in the presence of the Lord, the God of Israel. We cannot touch them. We must let them live, for God would be angry with us if we broke our oath."*
When leaders say they will do something, it is a binding commitment. They are not careless about their "verbal contracts."

Proverbs 15:1 *A gentle answer turns away wrath, but harsh words stir up anger.*
Words of blessing and wicked words are both very powerful.

Matthew 12:36-37 *I tell you this, that you must give an account on judgment day of every idle word you speak. The words you say now reflect your fate then; either*

you will be justified by them or you will be condemned.
The words you speak can condemn you or justify you on Judgment Day.

How can I lead best with my words?

Genesis 50:21 *And he spoke very kindly to them, reassuring them.*
Speak kind words to others.

Job 16:5 *I would speak in a way that helps you. I would try to take away your grief.*

Ephesians 4:29 *Let everything you say be good and helpful, so that your words will be an encouragement to those who hear them.*
Use words that build others up.

Proverbs 15:4 *Gentle words bring life and health.*

Proverbs 25:15 *Patience can persuade a prince, and soft speech can crush strong opposition.*
Speak to others with gentleness.

Proverbs 25:11 *Timely advice is as lovely as golden apples in a silver basket.*
When the time is right, giving good advice can be very beneficial.

Ecclesiastes 12:11 *A wise teacher's words spur students to action and emphasize important truths. The collected sayings of the wise are like guidance from a shepherd.*
Use words to instruct and inspire others to be wise.

1 Peter 3:9 *Don't repay evil for evil. Don't retaliate when people say unkind things about you. Instead, pay them back with a blessing. That is what God wants you to do, and he will bless you for it.*
Use your words to bless even those who injure you.

Zechariah 8:16 *But this is what you must do: Tell the truth to each other. Render verdicts in your courts that are just and that lead to peace.*
Speak truthfully.

What kinds of words should I avoid speaking?

Exodus 22:28 *Do not blaspheme God or curse anyone who rules over you.*
Never curse God or anyone in leadership (or in any other situation, for that matter).

Ecclesiastes 10:20 *Never make light of the king, even in your thoughts. And don't make fun of a rich man, either. A little bird may tell them what you have said.*
Do not mock or belittle those in leadership.

Psalm 34:12-13 *Do any of you want to live a life that is long and good? Then watch your tongue! Keep your lips from telling lies!*
Avoid saying anything that is deceptive or false.

Proverbs 18:8 *What dainty morsels rumors are—but they sink deep into one's heart.*
Avoid spreading gossip or slander about other people.

Proverbs 29:11 *A fool gives full vent to anger, but a wise person quietly holds it back.*
Avoid speaking in the heat of anger; you will usually regret it later.

James 4:11 *Don't speak evil against each other, my dear brothers and sisters. If you criticize each other and condemn each other, then you are criticizing and condemning God's law.*
Avoid criticizing other people.

PROMISES FROM GOD Proverbs 10:11 *The words of the godly lead to life.*

Proverbs 12:13 *The wicked are trapped by their own words, but the godly escape such trouble.*

Proverbs 20:15 *Wise speech is rarer and more valuable than gold and rubies.*

WORK

See also **BUSINESS, CALL OF GOD/CALLING, EMPLOYERS/EMPLOYEES**

How do leaders view work?

Genesis 1:27-28 *So God created people in his own image; God patterned them after himself; male and female he created them. God blessed them and told them, "Multiply and fill the earth and subdue it. Be masters over the fish and birds and all the animals."*

Wise leaders help those they lead understand the value and honor of work. God created us and gave us dominion over creation. In other words, God created us for work. Even before the curse, humanity was given the opportunity to transform the raw materials of earth into things that would enhance life. Work has always been meant to honor the Lord and bring us blessings.

Proverbs 13:11 *Wealth from get-rich-quick schemes quickly disappears; wealth from hard work grows.*

Honest, hard work is much better than schemes to get rich quickly.

Ecclesiastes 5:19 *To enjoy your work and accept your lot in life—that is indeed a gift from God.*

Colossians 3:17 *And whatever you do or say, let it be as a representative of the Lord Jesus, all the while giving thanks through him to God the Father.*
Your goal should be to work in such a way that you are a good representative of Christ.

1 Thessalonians 4:11-12 *This should be your ambition: to live a quiet life, minding your own business and working with your hands, just as we commanded you before. As a result, people who are not Christians will respect the way you live, and you will not need to depend on others to meet your financial needs.*
Your attitude toward work should include the goal of honoring God by the way you work, as well as supporting yourself.

What are the benefits of faithful work?
Proverbs 22:29 *Do you see any truly competent workers? They will serve kings rather than ordinary people.*

1 Kings 11:28 *Jeroboam was a very capable young man, and when Solomon saw how industrious he was, he put him in charge of the labor force from the tribes of Ephraim and Manasseh.*
Faithful work often brings opportunities to do more satisfying work.

Proverbs 10:4 *Lazy people are soon poor; hard workers get rich.*

Proverbs 12:11 *Hard work means prosperity; only fools idle away their time.*
Hard work usually yields the fruit of prosperity and success.

How should I do my work?
Proverbs 10:5 *A wise youth works hard all summer; a youth who sleeps away the hour of opportunity brings shame.*

Ecclesiastes 9:10 *Whatever you do, do well.*
Be industrious and do the best work you can when you have the opportunity.

Ecclesiastes 2:21 *I do my work with wisdom, knowledge, and skill.*

Romans 12:11 *Never be lazy in your work, but serve the Lord enthusiastically.*
Work with enthusiasm at whatever you do, keeping in mind that you are serving God, not people.

How do I deal with those who work poorly or will not work?
2 Thessalonians 3:11-12 *We hear that some of you are living idle lives, refusing to work and wasting time meddling in other people's business. In the name of the Lord Jesus Christ, we appeal to such people—no, we command them: Settle down and get to work. Earn your own living.*
Wise leaders confront those who refuse to work. This is not only necessary for the welfare of those who won't work, but also for fairness to those who do work. You must have the courage to speak the truth in love.

2 Thessalonians 3:6-13 *And now, dear brothers and sisters, we give you this command with the authority of our Lord Jesus Christ: Stay away from any Christian who lives in idleness and doesn't follow the tradition of hard work we gave you. For you know that you ought to follow our example. We were never lazy when we were with you. We never accepted food from anyone without paying for it.*

We worked hard day and night so that we would not be a burden to any of you. It wasn't that we didn't have the right to ask you to feed us, but we wanted to give you an example to follow. Even while we were with you, we gave you this rule: "Whoever does not work should not eat." Yet we hear that some of you are living idle lives, refusing to work and wasting time meddling in other people's business. In the name of the Lord Jesus Christ, we appeal to such people—no, we command them: Settle down and get to work. Earn your own living. And I say to the rest of you, dear brothers and sisters, never get tired of doing good.

Wise leaders can learn much from this classic model of confrontation. Paul first states the authority that lies behind his exhortation. Second, he appeals to his own example and integrity. Then he describes the consequences of failing to heed his counsel. You are responsible to those you lead, but you cannot take responsibility away from those who refuse to be led.

Proverbs 26:13-16 *The lazy person is full of excuses, saying, "I can't go outside because there might be a lion on the road! Yes, I'm sure there's a lion out there!" As a door turns back and forth on its hinges, so the lazy person turns over in bed. Some people are so lazy that they won't lift a finger to feed themselves. Lazy people consider themselves smarter than seven wise counselors.*

Often lazy people will refuse to listen to any advice. In fact, they may offer the most absurd rationalizations to try to justify their laziness. Again, leaders are responsible to those they lead, but they cannot take responsibility away from those who refuse to be led. Those who refuse wise counsel must be allowed to suffer the consequences of their choices.

Can I work too hard?

Psalm 39:6 *All our busy rushing ends in nothing.*

Ecclesiastes 5:3 *Just as being too busy gives you nightmares . . .*
While you are called to work hard, you must make sure that your work doesn't so preoccupy you that you endanger your health, your relationships, or your time with God.

Acts 16:16 *She was a fortune-teller who earned a lot of money for her masters.*
You must make sure that you don't allow your work to compromise your values.

Exodus 16:23 *The Lord has appointed tomorrow as a day of rest.*

Mark 6:31 *Then Jesus said, "Let's get away from the crowds for a while and rest."*
There is a time to stop your work in order to rest, to celebrate, and to worship God.

PROMISE FROM GOD Colossians 3:23-24 *Work hard and cheerfully at whatever you do, as though you were working for the Lord rather than for people. . . . The Lord will give you an inheritance as your reward.*

WORRY

How does worry touch a leader's life?

Exodus 15:24-25 *Then the people turned against Moses. "What are we going to drink?" they demanded. So Moses cried out to the Lord for help.*
People sometimes get overwhelmed and take their

anxiety out on the leader. Wise leaders, like Moses, must be able to recognize the anxiety for what it is so that they can respond appropriately to lessen the anxiety.

2 Corinthians 11:28-29 *Then, besides all this, I have the daily burden of how the churches are getting along. Who is weak without my feeling that weakness? Who is led astray, and I do not burn with anger?*
Leaders carry the burden of care for their group or organization. This burden can be either an occasion for worry or an opportunity for trust.

What do I do with my worry?
1 Peter 5:7 *Give all your worries and cares to God, for he cares about what happens to you.*

Philippians 4:6 *Don't worry about anything; instead, pray about everything.*
The first step in dealing with worry is to release it to the Lord in prayer. Hand it off to him as if to a consultant you totally trust, as if to a supervisor you have the utmost confidence in.

Colossians 3:2 *Let heaven fill your thoughts. Do not think only about things down here on earth.*

Philippians 4:8-9 *And now, dear brothers and sisters, let me say one more thing as I close this letter. Fix your thoughts on what is true and honorable and right. Think about things that are pure and lovely and admirable. Think about things that are excellent and worthy of praise. Keep putting into practice all you learned from me and heard from me and saw me doing, and the God of peace will be with you.*
The second step in dealing with worry is to fix your thoughts on the power of God, not the problems of

life. Turn your attention away from negative, unbelieving thoughts to the positive, constructive thoughts of faith, hope, and love.

Exodus 14:13 *But Moses told the people, "Don't be afraid. Just stand where you are and watch the Lord rescue you."*

The third step in dealing with worry is to instruct those you lead in the ways of faith and trust. Combat worry and anxiety by remembering and trusting God's promises.

PROMISE FROM GOD Psalm 55:22 *Give your burdens to the Lord, and he will take care of you.*

WORSHIP

See also **SABBATH**

What is the ultimate purpose of worship?

1 Chronicles 29:10-13 *Then David praised the Lord in the presence of the whole assembly: "O Lord, the God of our ancestor Israel, may you be praised forever and ever! Yours, O Lord, is the greatness, the power, the glory, the victory, and the majesty. Everything in the heavens and on earth is yours, O Lord, and this is your kingdom. We adore you as the one who is over all things. Riches and honor come from you alone, for you rule over everything. Power and might are in your hand, and it is at your discretion that people are made great and given strength. O our God, we thank you and praise your glorious name!"*

Isaiah 6:3 *In a great chorus they sang, "Holy, holy, holy is the Lord Almighty! The whole earth is filled with his glory!"*

Isaiah 66:1-2 *This is what the Lord says: "Heaven is my throne, and the earth is my footstool. Could you ever build me a temple as good as that? Could you build a dwelling place for me? My hands have made both heaven and earth, and they are mine. I, the Lord, have spoken! I will bless those who have humble and contrite hearts, who tremble at my word."*
Worship is the recognition of who God is, and of who you are in relation to him. It is your response to God's holiness, power, and grace. The greatest kings and leaders fall on their faces before the mighty Lord. Indeed, worship is the foundation and goal of effective leadership.

Exodus 23:19 *As you harvest each of your crops, bring me a choice sample of the first day's harvest. It must be offered to the Lord your God.*

Proverbs 3:9 *Honor the Lord with your wealth and with the best part of everything your land produces.*
Giving the firstfruits of your wealth and income is a part of your worship because it honors God.

Revelation 4:9-11 *Whenever the living beings give glory and honor and thanks to the one sitting on the throne, the one who lives forever and ever, the twenty-four elders fall down and worship the one who lives forever and ever. And they lay their crowns before the throne and say, "You are worthy, O Lord our God, to receive glory and honor and power. For you created everything, and it is for your pleasure that they exist and were created."*
Your worship of God is a foretaste of heaven.

What happens if I lose my focus on worship?
Deuteronomy 8:18-19 *Always remember that it is the Lord your God who gives you power to become rich, and he does it to fulfill the covenant he made with your*

ancestors. But I assure you of this: If you ever forget the Lord your God and follow other gods, worshiping and bowing down to them, you will certainly be destroyed. Those who refuse to honor God will not be honored by him. In fact, those who do not worship God will worship things that will lead to their destruction.

How do I make worship a part of my daily life?

JOHN 4:24 *God is Spirit, so those who worship him must worship in spirit and in truth.*
Worship is not confined to formal places and times. The only thing that is required is that you worship God in spirit (through authentic faith inspired by the Holy Spirit) and in truth (according to God's true person and nature). You can do that anytime and anywhere.

EPHESIANS 5:19 *Then you will sing psalms and hymns and spiritual songs among yourselves, making music to the Lord in your hearts.*
Worship, in addition to being an act of the people of God, is also a part of ordinary life. One way to bring worship into your daily life is through music—whether you sing it yourself or listen to it.

ROMANS 11:33-36 *Oh, what a wonderful God we have! How great are his riches and wisdom and knowledge! How impossible it is for us to understand his decisions and his methods! For who can know what the Lord is thinking? Who knows enough to be his counselor? And who could ever give him so much that he would have to pay it back? For everything comes from him; everything exists by his power and is intended for his glory. To him be glory evermore. Amen.*
Take time to praise God whenever you see his wisdom, power, direction, care, and love in your life. Worship then becomes a way of life.

PROMISES FROM GOD Psalm 66:4 *Everything on earth will worship you; they will sing your praises, shouting your name in glorious songs.*

Revelation 15:4 *Who will not fear, O Lord, and glorify your name? For you alone are holy. All nations will come and worship before you, for your righteous deeds have been revealed.*

Index

If you enjoyed *TouchPoints for Leaders*, you will love the *TouchPoint Bible*.

The *TouchPoint Bible* is the most helpful Bible available for finding just the right Bible verses to meet an immediate need in your life or in the life of someone you are trying to help. With the exclusive HelpFinder Index, you have instant access to hundreds of key topics and thousands of Bible verses. The *TouchPoint Bible* also includes book introductions and Bible promises as well as hundreds of in-text application notes to help you apply God's truth to everyday life. Make the *TouchPoint Bible* your favorite Bible for church, devotional reading, or study.